THE LOWBROW GUIDE TO

WORLD

HISTORY

W0008365

CASSELL
ILLUSTRATED

First published in Great Britain in 2005 by Cassell Illustrated,
A division of Octopus Publishing Group Limited,
2-4 Heron Quays, London E14 4JP

Publisher's note: The views expressed herein are the personal views of the author
and are not intended to reflect the views of the publisher.

© 2005 GUSTO COMPANY AS
Written by Michael Powell
Illustrations and Photography: Getty Images and Corbis Images
Executive Editor and original concept: James Tavendale
Edited by Katherine Robinson and Ewan Carpenter
Designed by Jeffrey Swartz

All rights reserved. No part of this publication may be reproduced, stored in a
retrieval system, or transmitted in any form or by any means, electronic, mechanical,
photocopying, recording, or otherwise, without the prior permission of the publisher.

A CIP catalogue record for this book is available from the British Library.

ISBN 1-84403-415-1
EAN 9781844034154

Printed in China

THE LOWBROW GUIDE TO
WORLD
HISTORY

CONTENTS

Did Dinosaurs' Testicles Lead to Mass Extinction? **10**

Tutankhamen: The King of Bling? **12**

The Trojan War **14**

Alexander the Not-So-Great **18**

Who Was the Biggest Nut-Job, Caligula or Nero? **22**

Vikings: Maritime Pioneers or Counter-Culture Kleptomaniacs? **26**

Who Would Win an Arm Wrestle: Attila the Hun
or Genghis Khan? **28**

A Brief History of Defecation **30**

The History of Toilet Paper **32**

William the Conqueror's Embarrassing Abscess **34**

From Myth to Monster: The Development of the Codpiece **36**

Precocious Brats Throughout Time **40**

Belt Up: Chastity in the Middle Ages **42**

Papal Bull: Ten Corrupt Popes **44**

Licking Leprosy: Why Kissing Sores Was Good
for Your Soul in the Middle Ages **48**

The Flagellants: Heaven Bent for Leather **50**

Seven Rulers and Their Food Fads **52**

Could Christopher Columbus Navigate
His Way out of a Paper Bag? **54**

Milestones in the History of Breasts **58**

Were the Conquistadors Stupid or What? **62**

Fat Chicks: A Historical Perspective **64**

Which of Henry VIII's Wives Was the Most Beddable? **68**

What Was So Terrible About Ivan?   **72**

Tulipmania   **74**

Ugly People Throughout the Ages   **76**

Thanks for Nothing: The Legacy of the Mayflower   **78**

The French Revolution   **80**

Napoleon: Ideologue, Opportunist,   **84**
or Annoying Little Corsican?

English King, 24, Impaled in a Gloucestershire Bathroom   **88**

Florence Nightingale: Lesbian Lady of the Night?   **92**

What's My Motivation, Love?   **94**

The Opium Wars: How Great Britain Created a Nation   **96**
of Junkies and Stole Hong Kong from the Chinese

Bring Me the Heads of Joaquin Murieta   **100**

American President Refuses to Be Photographed   **102**
in His Wheelchair

Sigmund Freud: The Cocaine Years   **104**

Suck It and See: The History of the Vacuum Cleaner   **108**

Huge Rocks and a Mother Complex: **112**
The Ego Behind the Making of Mount Rushmore

Was Gandhi Anorexic?   **114**

Great Moments in the History of Food   **116**

How Many Balls Did Hitler Have?   **120**

The Cold War According to Hollywood   **124**

Twelve Reasons Why Bill Gates Can Afford   **128**
to Wipe His Ass on George Washington's Face

Modern-Day Marvels   **132**

An Incomplete History of the Sexual Revolution   **136**

And Finally, Some Historical Anomalies   **140**

Index   **142**

INTRODUCTION

History can often seem meaningless, a confused heap of facts about a bunch of dead people—who bathed once a year and fought each other with obsolete weapons—with whom we have nothing in common. Yet how can we expect to understand and interpret the present and look to the future without referring to the past? As Kierkegaard said, "Life must be lived forward, but understood backwards." That's just the kind of penetrating, dialectic intelligence that you won't find in this book.

If history has taught us anything, it's that there's a lot of it around. In fact, we are privileged to live at a time when there's more of it than there has ever been. So why do we hate history? Maybe it's because there's just too much of it. No one on their deathbed ever said, "I wish I'd watched more documentaries."

This book sifts through the dates and dusty annals to bring history to a wider audience, and that includes you at the back, so wake up and maybe you'll discover that some of the past isn't so dull after all.

If you simplify it enough, history really boils down to four things: who killed who, who ruled who, who screwed who, and in what order. Once you've grasped this, it's easy to see that all those dead folk weren't so different from us. They wanted the same things. Okay, sometimes they wanted different things—like more teeth or not to have Bubonic plague—but, like us, they were driven by the twin desires: to stay alive and to get laid.

DID DINOSAURS' TESTICLES LEAD TO MASS EXTINCTION?

Nowadays we attribute the disappearance of the dinosaurs to the impact of a large comet or asteroid, which hit the earth 65 million years ago. We've all seen the documentaries showing the computer graphics re-creation of a sinister celestial object hurtling through space and breaking through the Earth's atmosphere before plunging into the Gulf of Mexico. Although that is currently the most widely accepted theory concerning dinosaur extinction, an earlier hypothesis laid the blame squarely (or rather roundly) on their gonads.

In a 1946 edition of the *Bulletin of the American Museum of Natural History*, three reptile fossil experts, E. H. Colbert, R. B. Cowles, and C. M. Bogert, published an article about temperature tolerances in American alligators. They had spent the last few years sticking rectal thermometers where the sun don't shine while avoiding permanent disfigurement by irate gators. They then attempted to extrapolate the data to make wild and completely untestable claims about dino balls.

Three hundred years earlier, Galileo had come up with a

theory about the unequal scaling of area versus volume. When an object (or animal) increases in size, its volume (being in three dimensions) grows much faster than its area (two dimensions). Therefore, small animals have much more skin relative to the volume of their flesh than larger ones. Enormous animals like dinosaurs would have had a much smaller proportion of skin to flesh. Since animals lose a lot of heat through their skin, it follows that the larger an animal is, the longer it will take to absorb or lose heat through its surface area (skin).

Fast forward to 1946; Colbert, Cowles, and Bogert compared the rates at which small and large alligators warmed and cooled down. They found that a teeny tiny alligator weighing one-tenth of a pound heated up one degree Celsius (1.8 degrees Fahrenheit) every 90 seconds, while a larger alligator weighing 29 pounds took more than five times longer. They calculated that a ten-ton dinosaur would have taken 86 hours to warm up one degree Celsius! They combined this with the knowledge that there was a world temperature rise before the Cretaceous extinction, to suggest that global warming sterilized the larger dinosaurs because their testicles (which are notoriously susceptible to fluctuations in temperature) were unable to operate in the new climate.

Unfortunately, as evolutionary biologist Stephen Jay Gould has pointed out, this is a totally useless hypothesis – it cannot be tested since "testicles simply don't fossilize, and how could we infer their temperature tolerances even if they did?" He concludes that the hypothesis is "only an intriguing speculation leading nowhere." Who said the history of science lacks balls?

TUTANKHAMEN:
THE KING OF BLING?

The phrase "bling bling" now appears in the new Oxford English Dictionary, marking the end of its brief journey from street slang to mainstream usage.

But that is not to say that the tradition of adorning one's body with ostentatious displays of heavy and expensive jewelry has its origins solely in the hip-hop culture that in turn traces its roots to the block parties of the Bronx in the seventies. To find the true granddaddy of bling, we must look even further back to ancient Egypt.

Inside lay Tutankhamen, wearing his famous gold mask.

King Tutankhamen was in his late teens when he died, and was buried along with the entire contents of his bedroom over 3,000 years ago. It was only in 1922, when Egyptologist Howard Carter excavated in the Valley of the Kings that this remarkable treasure trove was uncovered.

The burial chamber itself contained four gilded shrines, one inside the other, and built over a stone sarcophagus.

Nested together were three coffins, the innermost made of solid gold. Inside lay Tutankhamen, wearing his famous gold mask.

Next to the burial chamber was the treasury housing all his precious belongings. (The ancient Egyptians believed that they could take their personal effects into the next world.)

Much has been made of the Pharaoh's curse after Lord Carnarvon, Carter's sponsor, died from an infected mosquito bite a few weeks after the shrine was discovered. When Howard Carter's pet canary got eaten by a cobra, a powerful symbol of protection to the Pharaohs, no further proof seemed necessary, despite the rather obvious fact that snakes like to eat small birds.

But conclusive evidence of the tenacity of the curse surely came in 1980, after the untimely death of Lady Evelyn Herbert, Lord Carnarvon's daughter and one of the first into the tomb. She was just 79 years old.

THE TROJAN WAR

Adecade-long epic struggle over a woman, between the Greeks (no sense of direction) and the Trojans (gullible fools), which the Greeks eventually won.

It all began at the wedding of Peleus (Achilles's father) and Thetis (a sea nymph). They left Eris, the goddess of discord, off the guest list. She turned up anyway, but she didn't cause trouble in the conventional way by making out with the groom, drinking the wedding dry, and passing out in a floral arrangement. Instead, she placed a golden apple on the table and said whichever goddess was the most beautiful could have it.

The room was full of A-list deities, so it was no surprise that three of them reached for the apple at the same time. They were Hera (the goddess of marriage, said to restore her hymen each year by bathing in a sacred spring), Aphrodite (the goddess of love and a major-league tramp who cheated on her husband with Ares, Hermes, Poseidon, and Dionysus), and Athena (the goddess of wisdom and knitting, a babe with a magic goatskin breastplate, fringed with serpents, that generated thunderbolts whenever she shimmied).

Since Hera was Zeus's wife and the other two his daughters, he gave Paris, supposedly the most gorgeous hunk on earth, the task of judging. The goddesses all tried to bribe him: Hera

It all began at the wedding of Peleus and Thetis. They left Eris, the goddess of discord, off the guest list. She turned up anyway.

offered him power, Athena promised him riches, and Aphrodite tempted him with the most beautiful woman in the world. Naturally he chose the latter, Helen of Troy, the product of a one-night stand between Zeus and a swan (the gods really knew how to live!). But Helen was already married to Menelaus, the king of Sparta, so Paris sailed there to claim his prize. Menelaus entertained him lavishly, but as soon as his back was turned Paris hoofed it to Troy with Helen and lots of the king's stuff.

Menelaus summoned the Helen appreciation society—a bunch of her former boyfriends who had long ago vowed to defend her honour should the need arise. Most of them had other things to worry about and didn't want to go. Odysseus pretended to be mad and Achilles, who had been disguised as a girl by his parents, was tricked into going by Odysseus.

The Greek fleet of a thousand ships (Helen's was the face that launched them) couldn't set sail because the leader Agamemnon had vexed the goddess Diana, so he had to knock off his daughter Iphigenia before Diana would rustle up a favourable wind. Then the fleet got lost, laid siege to the wrong city, and returned home empty handed. Achilles finally asked directions from King Telephus and they set sail again.

Then they built a huge wooden horse, which was hollow inside, filled it with Greek soldiers, and left it outside the gates of Troy.

The ensuing war went on for ten years. The Greeks devastated the Trojans. They wasted the Trojan hero Hector, mutilated the corpse, tied it to his chariot, and dragged it away. But Achilles was killed by Paris (after first being wounded by an arrow in his Achilles's heel—what were the chances of that?).

They had yet to breach the walls of Troy. Odysseus had captured a prophet called Helenus who told the Greeks that Troy would only fall if four key indicators were met: They must persuade Achilles' son Pyrrhus to join their posse (which they did); they must use the bow and arrows that belonged to Hercules (one of their crew, Philoctetes, had them, but he had been left in Lemnos with a smelly snake bite, so they put

clothespins on their noses and fetched him back); they had to bring the rotting remains of Pelops to Troy (which they did); and finally, Odysseus had to steal a statue of Athena.

Then they built a huge wooden horse, which was hollow inside, filled it with Greek soldiers, and left it outside the gates of Troy. When the Greek fleet sailed away, the Trojans thought they had surrendered and dragged the horse into the city, only to be slaughtered that evening by the hidden warriors.

The Greeks were victorious, but the shine was taken off their success when some of them got hugely lost again. Odysseus, for one, spent a decade trying to find his way back to Ithaca (Homer's Odyssey tells the story of this eventful homeward journey).

ALEXANDER
THE NOT-SO-GREAT

Son of the whoring, alcoholic King Phillip II of Macedon, Alexander (356–323 B.C.) was less frivolous than his father, but was still a cross-dressing, stunted alcoholic with plenty to prove. He conquered the whole of the known world, demanded that he be worshipped as a god, and secured his place in history far above all the other classical greats. How many Macedonian legends can boast an appearance in the Koran and being played by Colin Farrell, Richard Burton, and William Shatner?

What drove him in his conquests? Certainly as a kid he must have been embarrassed by his dad, who was a coarse, uneducated barbarian with a drinking problem who had flagrant and very public affairs. Dad had one eye missing and his nose had been broken many times. Alexander's parents hated each other. His mother Olympus was from better stock than his father, being descended not only from the King of Epirus, but also possibly from the greatest fighter in history, Achilles, who was

Alexander's biggest hero. But even she was totally eccentric with suspect habits. Deeply religious, she was the high priestess of a cult and kept snakes in her bedroom. She hated Alexander's father so much that she told him that she had been

impregnated by Zeus in the form of a serpent.

After a traumatic childhood, living in a warring household in a warring country, it is not surprising that Alexander, like most teenagers, couldn't wait to leave home, disown his parents, and conquer the world.

Alexander did benefit from an education, albeit a particularly brutal one. From the age of seven he was taught by his mother's uncle, Leonidas, a sadistic bastard who spent years toughening him up and teaching him survival techniques. His "training," which included lots of push-ups and a starvation diet,

It is not surprising that Alexander, like most teenagers, couldn't wait to leave home, disown his parents, and conquer the world.

was so extreme that it stunted Alexander's growth. Years later, despite conquering most of the known world—including Gaza, the spice capital of the Middle East—he was unable still to put behind him a painful and vivid memory from his childhood when Leonidas had scolded him for putting too much incense on his burnt offering. To get back at his old mentor, Alexander arranged for eighteen tons of frankincense and myrrh to be dumped on the teacher's front lawn in what was surely the most misplaced and expensive "screw-you" gesture of all time. Alexander the Grudge anyone? Leonidas must have felt like he'd won the lottery. In his case, he actually succeeded.

Later, Aristotle (before he became famous) was his tutor for three years and taught him how to think philosophically and tactically and how slavery was a normal, healthy thing. Unfortunately his father pulled him out of school early to put

It should be stressed that while Alexander was a gifted soldier, he didn't create his empire from scratch; he inherited a very healthy family business.

down a rebellion. So, at age 16, while most of his friends were playing with toy soldiers, he had his first taste of victory and founded his first small city, Alexandropolis.

It should be stressed that while Alexander was a gifted soldier and tactician, he didn't create his empire from scratch; he inherited a very healthy family business. While Alexander was growing up, his father was busy conquering much of Greece. In fact, he'd have to be a complete loser not to since Persia was well in decline. This annoyed the young Alexander who sulked, "My father will have everything, and I will have nothing left to conquer." When Alexander took over, Macedonia already had a strong economy and a huge army. He just had to point it in the right direction.

When Alexander's gay lover Hephaestion died, he went on a bender of "sacrificing and drinking," which seems to have sent him into a spiral of bingeing and cross-dressing (as the goddess Artemis) that weakened his body so much he died of malaria and a liver infection at the age of 33.

WHO WAS THE BIGGEST NUT-JOB, CALIGULA OR NERO?

Caligula was Nero's uncle and in the mad-god-complex-screw-your-sisters-and-kill-your-parents-eat-till-you-puke tradition of Roman emperors, they didn't come much crazier than this pair. Below is a list of their top ten shortcomings.

Gaius "Caligula" (A.D. 12–41)

1. He was so sensitive about his baldness that he made it a capital crime to look down on him from a high place. He ordered anyone who had nice hair to have it shaved off. Mullets were punishable by death.

2. When he ran out of criminals to feed to the lions, he had spectators dragged out of the crowd and thrown into the arena.

3. He appointed his horse, Incitatus, a priest of his temple and tried to have it made a senator. He bought it jewels, furniture,

statues, and its own servants.

4. He dissolved pearls in vinegar and then drank the brew.

5. One of his favourite hobbies was rolling around on piles of gold.

6. He forced rich people to leave their estates to him in their wills, then had them murdered.

7. He marched an army to the northern shore of France so that he could pick seashells which he called the "spoils of the conquered ocean."

8. He committed incest with his three sisters.

9. He got his sister Drusilla pregnant and, convinced the baby was a god, ripped it from her womb with his own hands.

He got his sister pregnant and, convinced the baby was a god, ripped it from her womb with his own hands.

10. He demanded that he be worshipped as a god. He had a temple to himself built complete with a life-sized gold statue of himself, which was dressed each day in the same clothes that he was wearing.

"Nero" Claudius Caesar (A.D. 37–68)

1. He attempted to kill his mother Agrippina by sending her on a journey in a booby-trapped ship. She swam to safety, so he had her killed anyway and then got Seneca to trash her reputation with his writing.

2. He had a sexual relationship with a man called Doryphorus because he looked like his mother.

3. He dressed in disguise and walked around Rome beating up passers by.

4. He killed his pregnant wife, Sabina Poppaea (who also resembled his mother), by kicking her in the stomach.

5. After Sabina's death he transferred his affections to a young man called Sporus, who looked like Sabina. He had him castrated to complete the illusion, married him, dressed him in her clothes, and gave him the nickname "Sabina."

6. He had a crush on the actor Paris, who gave him acting lessons, but had him killed for being a better actor than him (and not looking enough like his mother).

7. He used to lock citizens in theatres and force them to watch his own performances of singing and tiresome recitals of epic poems.

8. He is rumoured to have started the great fire of Rome in A.D. 64 to make way for an extension to his palace.

He used to lock citizens in theatres and force them to watch his own performances of singing and recitals of epic poems.

9. He took part in all the events at the Olympic games and bribed the judges so that he won every single one.

10. He committed suicide by stabbing himself in the neck. His last words were "Oh, what an artist the world is losing!"

VIKINGS:

MARITIME PIONEERS OR
COUNTER-CULTURE KLEPTOMANIACS?

The venturesome seafarers we know today as the Vikings came from Denmark, Norway, and Sweden, and spread through Europe and the North Atlantic for about 200 years between A.D. 800 and A.D. 1050 during what is known as the Viking Age.

Today their reputation is one of committing violence, creating mayhem, and practically discovering testosterone, which is unfair if you consider that Christian Europe spent the next three centuries brutally focused on their solemn vow to deliver the Holy Places from Muslim tyranny with unreasonable degrees of force. The Vikings didn't kill and loot in the name of the Pope or their religion. But they were honest in their motives—they wanted stuff and they were prepared to get in their boats to find it, at a time when everyone else in Europe was too chicken to sail out of sight of land.

The main source of the Vikings' fearsome reputation (as well as the misconception that they wore horned helmets) was in the stories, or "sagas," of great exploits that were passed down the generations orally; they were only written down centuries later by the very churchmen who had had their monasteries pillaged by the Vikings, so they were hardly objective sources.

They didn't wear horned helmets into battle—those were reserved for religious ceremonies.

Then as now, it is technology that triumphs in warfare. The majority of Vikings won fights not because they were superior warriors but because they were excellent sailors with hi-tech weaponry such as the double-edged sword and broad-leaved battle-axe, the Uzis and AK-47s of their time. Their flat-bottomed ships meant they could launch surprise attacks by sailing up shallow rivers, or right onto the shoreline, giving their victims little time to defend themselves. Also, they didn't wear horned helmets into battle—those were reserved for religious ceremonies.

However, there was a small group of extremely aggressive Vikings called the bezerkers who dressed in animal skins and had a reputation for fighting in a wild frenzy and being insensible to pain. Modern scholars believe they were high on amphetamines—hallucinogenic mushrooms such as Amanita muscaria—which corresponds with accounts of them grinding their teeth, biting the edge of their shields, and sucking dummies before going into battle to fight till dawn.

WHO WOULD WIN AN ARM WRESTLE: ATTILA THE HUN OR GENGHIS KHAN?

Attila the Hun (circa A.D. 406–453) was king of the Huns (the clue is in the name). He was one of the most feared and notorious barbarians who ever lived. Genghis Khan was born in the early 1160s and established the largest empire ever. It ranged from the Caspian Sea to the Sea of Japan.

Attila was probably the bigger nutcase of the two. His claim to have discovered the actual sword of Mars is the sort of tall story only a deluded psychopath would expect people to believe. When he wasn't rolling his eyes, nobody could look into them without flinching. He also murdered his brother and is alleged to have eaten two of his sons, although that may be because one of his wives served them up to him in revenge.

He also murdered his brother and is alleged to have eaten two of his sons, although that may be because one of his wives served them up to him in revenge.

Genghis was probably the greater tactician of the two, but since his father was poisoned when Genghis was just a boy of ten, he must have had his fair share of anger-management issues, though at least there are historical accounts which credit him with the kind of sensitivity that it's hard to imagine Attila possessing. When he passed through the Ordos area of North

China during his final battle campaign, he liked the view so much that he dropped his horsewhip and announced that he would like to be buried there (after his death). So his attendants promptly buried his horsewhip on the spot and erected a ceremonial stone over it (records don't mention whether Genghis found this pleasing or rather irritating). Since the early Qing dynasty there has been a shrine to Genghis's memory at this site.

Since arm wrestling is as much about tactics as brute strength, it is likely that Genghis would keep a cooler head and kick Attila's ass. But then the Scourge of God would probably follow him into the toilet and cut his head off while he was doing his business.

A BRIEF HISTORY
OF DEFECATION

4000–2500 B.C.

Babylonians have storm water drain systems and cesspools in some larger homes. No toilet brushes were discovered during excavation.

2500 B.C.

Sitting toilets appear and then disappear again with the fortunes of the ancient Indus people. The Harappa civilization in India has water-flushed toilets in each house and a sewage system with manhole covers. Archaeological evidence of this system has been uncovered at Lothal in Western India.

1700 B.C.

Flush toilets reappear in Crete, with extravagant bathrooms and elaborate bejeweled plumbing systems. The Minoan Palace of Knossos boasts four separate drainage systems and great stone sewers.

800 B.C.–A.D. 300

The Cloaca Maxima, the first sewers of Rome, are built and still provide run-off drainage for the city today. The Dejecti Effusive Act is introduced, compensating those hit or injured by flying feces thrown from windows during daylight hours.

A.D. 500–1500

The fecal dark ages. A time of cesspools, doing it in the street, and throwing it out of the window or into the river. People perform their business wherever they are caught short, then feed it to their pigs.

1596

Sir John Harrington invents a toilet (which he names a "water closet") for his godmother, Queen Elizabeth I. It doesn't catch on. Elizabeth continues to hurl crap from the windows of Hampton Court Palace.

1775

London watchmaker Alexander Cummings reinvents the toilet, and introduces the "S" bend. It proves an ineffective means of telling the time.

1857

Joseph Cayetty invents toilet paper. Twenty-nine years later, New York holds its first ticker tape parade.

1859

In London, the polluted Thames has become a cesspool. In the hot summer, Parliament is suspended because of the foul stench.

1861–1904

Thomas Crapper does not invent the toilet, but does take out nine plumbing patents including the Silent Valveless Water Waste Preventer and mistakenly goes down in posterity as the progenitor of the word "crap."

T HE HISTORY OF TOILET PAPER

Humankind is nothing if not resourceful. Before toilet paper became commonplace, a variety of alternatives were used: sheep's wool (Vikings); a sponge on the end of a stick (Romans); hay balls or a scraper called a gompf stick (Middle Ages); corn cobs (Pilgrims); left hands (India and the Middle East); coconut shells (Hawaii); and lace (French aristocracy).

However, if you have ever wondered when we made the switch to toilet paper, you may be surprised to learn that a fastidious fourteenth-century Chinese emperor commissioned huge sheets of t.p. with an area of about six square feet. It isn't known whether he was a scruncher or folder, but he clearly took his ablutions seriously, since the Bureau of Imperial Supplies made 720,000 sheets each year.

But it wasn't until the mid-nineteenth century that bathroom tissue became commercially available. In 1857 Joseph C. Gayetty produced the world's first packets of bathroom tissue, which he called "therapeutic paper." Packs contained 500 sheets, each one proudly bearing the name of its inventor.

Within 20 years it was on a roll—literally—manufactured by the Scott Paper Company. Founded in 1879 by brothers E. Irvin and Clarence Scott in Philadelphia, Scott Paper was the leading toilet paper company in the world by 1925. Although attending to one's backside was a difficult subject, early ads warned that "harsh toilet tissue may cause serious injury" and played up the health benefits of their softer brand that was impregnated with aloe and contained "thirsty fibres." Nowadays Kimberly-Clark is the biggest manufacturer since it acquired Scott in 1995 (Charles Benjamin Clark, a 28-year-old Civil War veteran, teamed up with John A. Kimberly and built their first paper mill in Wisconsin in 1872).

But the paper wasn't what you'd call soft by modern standards—it was single ply and fairly inflexible. The first truly soft two-ply toilet paper was made in 1942 by St. Andrew's Paper Mill in Walthamstow, London. Mention should be made of Kimberly-Clark's 1944 "E" Award for commercial excellence for its valiant effort to keep World War II soldiers clean and fresh. And who can forget Johnny Carson's ill-judged joke about a toilet paper shortage in 1973 that caused such a run on the market (so to speak) as people rushed out to the shops to stockpile that he had to calm the buying frenzy with a hasty public apology.

Since then humankind has made huge strides in softness, strength, absorbency, and availability. In 2001 Kimberly-Clark launched Cottonelle Fresh™ Rollwipes—America's first premoistened wipe on a roll.

Can things get any better? Paper with a built in smart chip—now that would really be something worth wiping for.

WILLIAM THE CONQUEROR'S EMBARRASSING ABSCESS

William is famous for his opportunistic trip to England in 1066 to take advantage of the disputed succession. It is also well known that he defeated King Harold at The Battle of Hastings and then started building castles everywhere like they were going out of fashion. A thousand years later, British taxpayers are still being fleeced in a futile attempt to prevent these shoddily built heritage slums from collapsing. (Before he earned his fearsome-warrior moniker, he was known as "William the Bastard" because he was the illegitimate son of the Duke of Normandy.) What is often forgotten is that his funeral was one of the most distasteful royal send-offs ever recorded.

He died as he had lived: stealing and fighting. He was injured while sacking the town of Mantes, the wound became infected, and it killed him on September 9, 1087, at the age of sixty. After his death, the abscess continued to grow, owing to the build-up of gases and post-mortem swelling of his body.

He had also grown very fat in his later years (earning him the nickname "William the Fat Bastard"), so when his corpse was brought to the church of St. Stephen at Caen, it proved a significant challenge for his attendants who were unable to

Before he earned his fearsome-warrior moniker, he was known as "William the Bastard" because he was the illegitimate son of the Duke of Normandy.

lay him to rest in his stone sarcophagus. When a group of bishops pressed down on his body, the abscess burst, sending pus and rotting flesh everywhere and filling the church with an unbearable stench. Mourners fled in chaos, vomiting into their handkerchiefs as they trampled each other in their scramble for the exit.

FROM MYTH TO MONSTER: THE DEVELOPMENT OF THE CODPIECE

It is comforting to know that women aren't the only victims of fashion blunders. From its humble origins in the Middle Ages to the confident thrusting behemoths of the High Renaissance, the development of the codpiece shows that men, too, can make themselves look like donkeys. But before you get too smug, where do you think your necktie is pointing?

Originally it was simply a triangular pouch or braguette designed to cover the "cod" (scrotum) but its subsequent growth was linked to several factors: the length of men's doublets, the personality of successive kings, the strategies of war, and above all, the need for a guy to gain easy access to his private parts.

At the beginning of the thirteenth century men wore a doublet (like a skirt) and hose (leggings that ended at the crotch). Nobody saw much need to cover the genitals, since they were mostly hidden under the hose. Someone might catch a glimpse when you were mounting your horse or kicking a peasant, but no one really cared, except the Church.

By the fourteenth century, Edward III was busy fighting the Hundred Years' War to stake his claim on the French throne, and legend has it that he

The development of the codpeice shows that men, too, can make themselves look like donkeys.

had the codpiece on his armour enlarged to scare the enemy. An army might march on its belly, but fighting prowess was thought to lie further south. He ordered that the nobility and his knights follow his example. Chinese whispers among the French troops must have led to some interesting misunderstandings: "Mon Dieu! Have you heard? The English have developed a longer loaf—we'd better get baking!"

Whether or not this myth is true, by the first half of the fifteenth century, it is unlikely that the pious king Henry V or his inept son Henry VI would have wanted to draw attention to their family jewels, but something would have to be done soon, since doublets were getting shorter and shorter. It wasn't until Henry VI lost his throne to the young and thrusting Plantagenet dreamboat, Edward IV, that the codpiece really took off. Allegedly one of the sexiest men in Europe, he brought the feel-good factor back to England. And, as every economist knows, when a country becomes more prosperous, inflationary pressures increase. English nobles literally swelled with pride. If the teenage king had owned a Ford Mustang instead of a horse, he would have added spoilers, UV strips, and side skirts. But in the absence of these, he put all his attention into customizing his knob.

But just when it seemed that codpieces were reaching new heights, the first Tudor king, Henry VII, came along and popped the bubble. He was not a handsome man. Doublets

If the teenage king had owned a Ford Mustang instead of a horse, he would have added spoilers, UV strips, and side skirts.

lengthened and codpieces became flaccid again. Fortunately he only ruled for 24 years after which his son Henry VIII injected a new impetus: his specimen was hugely padded and covered in jewels. It was during his reign that coddies developed into full-blown Renaissance monsters. With good reason—syphilis was rife and not only did a large codpiece double as a hip bag; it also hid layers of medicated bandages. In Henry's case it also over-compensated for his inability to produce a male heir.

Then began their inevitable decline when his daughter Elizabeth I took the throne. She never married and clearly didn't want the nobility reminding her by parading huge members in front of her face. The Spanish were flushed with their conquests and were sailing around the New World sporting permanent erections, but they were the exception. The effeminate French king Henry III killed off the codpiece in France and it wasn't long before European men were mincing around with earrings. By the end of the sixteenth century, the most absurd fashion statement the world had ever seen had been given its pink slip.

PRECOCIOUS BRATS
THROUGHOUT TIME

If you think that Mozart was advanced for his age, check out some of the achievements that other gifted babies and toddlers have made. It makes you reflect on how much time Wolfgang wasted in those early years.

5 seconds old
With a little help from her older half-brother Hephaestus and a large axe, Athena springs from the head of her father Zeus already full grown and dressed in a set of armour (Zeus had earlier swallowed her mother Metis).

1 minute old
On July 25, 1978, Louise Brown becomes world famous as the first successful "test tube" baby before her umbilical cord has even been cut.

12 hours old
Hermes climbs out of his cradle and steals a herd of cattle belonging to Apollo. A few hours later he makes the world's first lute out of the shell of a tortoise and appeases Apollo by teaching him how to play it.

5 days old
Prince Siddhartha is examined by eight learned men and impresses them so much that they correctly predict he will grow up to become a Buddha.

1 week old

Mary Queen of Scots becomes Queen of Scotland on December 7, 1542, after the death of her father. She is crowned nine months later at Stirling Castle on September 9, 1543.

6 months old

Hercules strangles two snakes that have been put in his crib by his father's jealous wife, Hera.

Age 3

Shirley Temple makes her first Baby Burlesk films. In 1934, at the age of five she wins an Oscar for singing "On the Good Ship Lollipop." By the age of six, she has made 20 of her 44 films.

Sigmund Freud is sexually aroused by seeing his mother naked.

Age 4

Michael Jackson becomes the lead vocalist and frontman of the Jackson 5 (1964).

Age 5

Wolfgang Amadeus Mozart finally gets around to writing his first composition (1761) and tours the courts of Europe giving recitals on the clavier, violin, and organ. At age six he writes the famous twelve variations on the tune *"Twinkle, Twinkle Little Star."* What a slacker.

BELT UP:
CHASTITY IN THE MIDDLE AGES

Chastity belts have been the subject of jokes and ribald stories since the Crusades. It is hard to imagine a world of knights and their ladies without being reminded of their obsession with obedience, loyalty, and chastity. But when did chastity belts make their first appearance?

Today, the earliest surviving specimens are kept in the Cluny Museum in Paris. One is a beguiling mixture of ivory, velvet, and cold iron, originally believed to date to the late sixteenth century, but this has recently been exposed as a nineteenth-century fake; the second specimen dates to the seventeenth century and, while it skimps on the velvet, the iron plates are decked out in gold and are decorated with a charming scene of Adam and Eve in the Garden of Eden. Both specimens are well-made and expertly crafted.

The first mention of a chastity belt in literature appears in an obscure French epic poem written by Marie de France in the twelfth century. A knight and his paramour tie shirts around their nether regions using a complicated system of knots that cannot be undone, making removal impossible

The first mention of a chastity belt in literature appears in an obscure French epic poem written by Marie de France in the twelfth century.

without cutting the garments. They then pledge fidelity and the knight rides off to the Crusades, no doubt feeling very smug until the first time he dismounts and squats behind a tree.

The earliest illustration of a chastity belt appears in a military encyclopedia called the Bellifortis, written by Konrad Kyeser von Eichstadt in 1405. It shows a clumsy and heavy contraption that was made out of iron and could be locked.

In the fifteenth century an Italian judge called Francesco de Carerra introduced the "fibula" to Europe, which involved inserting a piece of metal or ivory through the pierced genitals. He used it to lock up all his mistresses and subsequently became so unpopular that he was later found strangled.

But women weren't the only ones to suffer "infibulation." The male equivalent in which the foreskin is pulled over the head, pierced, and secured was very popular amongst comic actors and musicians in ancient Rome who believed that celibacy would improve their voices.

PAPAL BULL:
TEN CORRUPT POPES

Stephen VII (b. unknown; pope 896–897)

This sicko had the rotting corpse of his predecessor and sworn enemy, Pope Formosus, dug up and subjected to a mock trial (the Cadaver Synod) in which he was found guilty of coveting the papal throne. The corpse was then "punished" by being stripped, having three fingers removed, and then being dumped into the river Tiber. Stephen was later imprisoned and strangled to death.

Urban II (b. 1042; pope 1088–1099)

He decreed that married priests who ignored the celibacy laws be imprisoned for the good of their souls. He had the wives and children of those married priests sold into slavery. Also started the First Crusade in 1095.

Gregory IX (b. 1145; pope 1227–1241)

The pope who, in 1231, established the Inquisition for the apprehension and trial of heretics (i.e., non-Catholics). Say no more.

Sixtus IV (b. 1414; pope 1471–1484)

Immediately after becoming pope he made two of his nephews cardinals and threw money and titles at numerous other relatives. He licensed the brothels in Rome, which generated an income of about 30,000 ducats a year, and he taxed

He was probably the most corrupt pope that ever lived; his wickedness reached almost mythical status.

priests who had mistresses. Another of his scams involved selling indulgences for the dead: relatives would pay the church to reduce the suffering in purgatory of their deceased loved ones.

Innocent VIII (b. 1432; pope 1484–1492)

He was the first pope to acknowledge openly his illegitimate children, whom he showered with titles and married off into rich families. He made his 13-year-old grandson a cardinal. His papal bull Summis desiderantes (1484) created the Inquisition in Germany to seek, torture, and destroy witches.

Alexander VI (b.1431; pope 1492–1503)

Probably the most corrupt pope that has ever lived; his wickedness reached almost mythical status. Born Rodrigo Borgia, he rose through the church through nepotism. His uncle Alfonso de Borgia (later Pope Calixtus III) showered him with ecclesiastical offices while he was still in his teens and made him a cardinal at age 25. As vice chancellor of the Roman Church, he became one of the world's richest men. He became pope through bribery (known as "simony"—a practice which he later banned), appointed 47 of his cronies as cardinals (including his teenage son, Cesare, and Alessandro Farnese—brother of his 19-year-old married mistress, Guilia Farnese—who later became Pope Paul III), committed adultery, murdered rivals, indulged in orgies, married off his daughter Lucrezia Borgia three times to form political alliances, and fathered seven children. You name it, he wrote the manual.

Leo X (b. 1475; pope 1513–1521)

Nepotistic and obscenely extravagant, Leo (Giovanni de Medici) managed to bankrupt the papacy within two years and spent the rest of his papacy selling ecclesiastical jobs and indulgences and pawning palace furniture to support his lavish lifestyle. His rationale was "Let us enjoy the papacy since God has given it to us." In Raphael's celebrated picture at the Pitti Gallery in Florence, Leo is portrayed as fat and effeminate with beady little eyes. He had a reputation for being constantly sweaty and forever mopping his dripping brow. In his favour, he was a good-natured and generous patron of charity and the arts. He earned much of his income from licensing brothels (one out of every seven citizens in Rome at the time was a prostitute). It was this corruption that led Martin Luther to nail his 95 Theses on the church door in Wittenburg, thus starting the Protestant Reformation.

Paul III (b. 1468; pope 1534–1549)

Became a cardinal because his sister, Guilia, was having an affair with Pope Alexander VI (see over). His nepotism was immediately apparent—his first two cardinal appointments were his two young grandsons Alessandro Farnese (age 14) and Ascanio Sforza (age 16). He wasn't an out-and-out hedonist, but still had more than his fair share of illicit pleasure. He was the pope who excommunicated Henry VIII in 1538 for divorcing Catherine of Aragon.

Julius III (b. 1487; pope 1550–1555)

A typical Renaissance pope: nepotistic, pleasure-seeking, gluttonous, and an inveterate gambler. While pope he became infatuated with a 17-year-old boy, Innocenzo del Monte, whom he picked up while cruising the streets of Parma, and made him a cardinal.

Pious XII (b. 1876; pope 1939–1958)

Nicknamed "Hitler's Pope," when power-hungry Eugenio Pacelli became pontiff, he had already collaborated with Fascist leaders through his desire to promote papal absolutism, combined with his racism, anti-Semitism, and political and spiritual ambition. His diplomacy in Germany in the 1930s betrayed the very Catholic political associations that might have challenged Hitler's rise to power and prevented the Final Solution.

LICKING LEPROSY:

WHY KISSING SORES WAS GOOD FOR YOUR SOUL IN THE MIDDLE AGES

Leprosy is one of the oldest diseases in recorded history and is thought to have been referred to as early as 1552 B.C. in writings from an Egyptian papyrus. But what sets it apart from many other afflictions is the way it has been equated with moral rather than merely bodily corruption.

The Bible is obsessed with the disease. Leprosy is mentioned over fifty times, most notably in the story of Uzziah, the King of Judah, who was struck down with leprosy for being a disobedient little snot. All he did was light a few sticks of incense in the temple, which was apparently something only the priests were allowed to do. But back then God was a zero-tolerance deity who meted out some hefty punishments. Anyone remember the flood?

The New Testament is a little kinder on lepers—at least Jesus cured a few of them, but whereas he "heals" the deaf, he always seems to "cleanse" the poor old lepers—consolidating the theme of moral corruption.

By the Middle Ages, folk had developed a very ambivalent attitude towards lepers. Some medieval kings set a poor example—Philip V of France and Henry II of England had them burned at the stake without the last rites. But others thought that leprosy was a gift from God, since it meant that through earthly suffering they could atone for their sins, giving them a head start in purgatory and bumping them to the front of the queue at the pearly gates.

Also, at the beginning of the thirteenth century, St. Francis of Assisi had famously traded in his hedonistic life of luxury in favour of kissing lepers and washing their sores; many followed his example and the practice became very trendy. Before the arrival of the super-malls, what better way could there have been to spend your Sunday afternoon than take a picnic to the leper colony to suck it up and bank some heavenly credits?

But most people clung onto the traditional view that lepers were revolting sinners with anger management issues who harboured delusions that the

The Bible is obsessed with disease. Leprosy is mentioned over fifty times.

world was out to get them. Wouldn't you be a bit oversensitive if you'd had to forfeit all your possessions to your neighbours, take part in a mock funeral, and then be thrown out of your village wearing nothing but a black cloak, only to find that a crowd of do-gooders want to get intimate with your lesions?

Lepers also had a reputation for burning with carnal lusts. Go figure—your sex life takes a huge nose dive once the abscesses appear.

THE FLAGELLANTS:
HEAVEN BENT FOR LEATHER

Self-denial has always played an important role in religious observance, and the boundary between penitence and punishment has often been a little fuzzy, to say the least. However, a fanatical Italian sect, which flourished from the thirteenth century, brought this issue sharply into focus when they attempted to turn self-harm into a new religion. The Flagellants believed that beating yourself up was the best way to please God and get into heaven. So certain were they of this that they even took to assaulting Jews—presumably to save their souls as well.

Whipping had been the business among monastic orders for centuries. Saint Peter Damien is a well-documented eleventh-century scholar and S&M aficionado who regularly beat the crap out of himself and encouraged his monks to follow suit. The Dominicans and the Mendicants also enjoyed a fair bit of discipline, but it wasn't until 1260 that a Perugian Friar Raniero Fasani brought self-harming to a mass audience and made it something that everyone could enjoy. It didn't matter that you were a lay-person—all you needed was a low IQ and a big whip.

They formed into a sort of S&M travelling circus and staged great processions, involving anywhere from 200 to 10,000 people. They would march from town to town and put on miserable displays of public suffering, men and women stripped to the waist, beating the living daylights out of each other. It must have been a disturbing spectacle for the onlookers and a welcome diversion from the hardships of medieval life, not least the Black Death of 1259 that had made everyone either dead or noticeably edgy. They were convinced that the end of the world was coming, so watching or taking part in a flogfest was the closest these God-fearing peasants could get to actually humping in the streets.

Flagellation fever continued sporadically during the next century and was also very popular in Germany (no, really?). The ecclesiastical authorities weren't keen on it. They believed that punishment and making everyone feel guilty was the church's job, so several popes banned it. But by the mid-fourteenth century, the flagellant movement had become an organized sect calling themselves "Brotherhood of the Cross" and wearing white habits bearing a red cross.

Twice a day they would go to the local public square and strike a pose, depending on which sin they were having whipped out of them. For example, a perjurer would lie on his side with three fingers in the air while an adulterer would lie face down on the ground. After a damn good whipping one of them would read out a "letter from God" telling the crowd that inevitably gathered to atone for their sins.

It seemed that anywhere there was a crisis, like the next Plague outbreak in 1347, there'd also be corresponding crowds of self-harmers. They gradually died out as people tried out other fads, such as Jew-baiting and being crippled by St. Vitus Dance, although a few underground monastic orders do enjoy a spot of clandestine flogging even today.

SEVEN RULERS AND THEIR FOOD FADS

The Babylonian ruler **Nebuchadnezzar II** (605–562 B.C.) was a famous lunatic leader responsible for the exotic Hanging Gardens, but according to the Greek historian Herodotus, in later life he took to eating grass under the mistaken impression that he was, in fact, a goat.

The Roman Emperor **Vitellius** (A.D. 15–69) was such a glutton that he used to stick a feather down his throat between courses to make him puke, so that he could keep on eating. The Imperial Navy spent most of their time searching the seas for rare ingredients for his bizarre culinary creations, including pheasant brains, pike livers, and flamingo tongues. At one of his banquets more than 2,000 fish and 7,000 birds were on the menu. He eventually gave up being emperor so he could spend even more time pigging out.

A later Roman Emperor Marcus Aurelius Antoninus, better known as **Heliogabalus** (A.D. 204–222), is the epitome of an amoral aesthete. He thought it was a great practical joke to serve his guests exact replicas of whatever he was eating, made out of wood, wax, glass, ivory, pottery, and stone or napkins embroidered with pictures of food. He frequently ate camel heels and also cocks' combs taken from living birds, and he fed his dogs on goose livers. At one banquet he presented his guests with the heads of six hundred ostriches complete with brains. At another he dropped so many flowers from the false ceiling that some of his guests died from asphyxiation.

Chinese Emperor **Shih Hu** (A.D. 334–349) used to serve up his beheaded wives to his dinner guests and then pass the severed head around to prove that she wasn't coyote ugly. He thought it was hilarious to ask "Have you met my wife?"

The Holy Roman Emperor **Frederick II** (1194–1250) was a sicko who used to butcher his dinner guests so he could study the human digestive system.

Anne Boleyn (1507–1536) was bulimic. It was the duty of one of her ladies in waiting to hold up a sheet whenever she looked like she wanted to toss her cookies so not to bring too much attention to her yakking.

Portraits of **Louis XIV** (1638–1715) show him as a svelte little man, but he was actually a fat bastard. When he saw a pineapple for the first time he grabbed it and tried to bite through the prickly skin, cutting his lips. The foolish porker then outlawed pineapples in France. In his later years he had trouble eating because his incompetent dentists managed to smash his palate and upper jaw while removing some of his rotten teeth. He had difficulty chewing and food often used to spew out of his nose.

COULD CHRISTOPHER COLUMBUS NAVIGATE HIS WAY OUT OF A PAPER BAG?

The short answer is "no;" the long answer is "Look behind you—isn't that the Yangtze River?"

Everyone knows the rhyme "in 1492 Columbus sailed the ocean blue," but despite making four trips between 1492 and 1504, he never achieved his aim: to find a short cut to the Indies and to bring back untold riches. By the gold-hungry standards of his contemporaries, Columbus was a major-league screw up. He was also a liar.

Two hundred years earlier, his hero Marco Polo had returned from China to write a best-selling book with the understated title The Travels of Marco Polo, describing the great Kubla Khan and his exotic Mongol empire. It also detailed his encounters with headless men, dragons, unicorns, and a race of one-legged people with feet so large that they used them as umbrellas, (rather than hop under a tree for shelter, presumably). In this tradition, Columbus soon proved he, too, had no qualms about telling whoppers.

In the late fifteenth century, the uncharted Atlantic ocean was known as the "Sea of Darkness." It was thought that either hell or paradise, or both, could be found there. It was, after all, the place where the sun fell into the sea every evening, making the water boil. So, when he announced that the world might be round and he knew a better route to China, Spain held its breath, then everyone realized his great new scheme amounted to turning left after Africa rather than right, so they let out a big groan and went back to what they were doing—which largely consisted of taking the Bible at face value and carving furniture without pineapples.

By the gold-hungry standards of his contemporaries, Columbus was a major-league screw up. He was also a liar.

Everyone thought that at best he was mad and at worse, a dangerous heretic. It took him a good while to get decent sponsorship. When he approached Spanish monarchs, Ferdinand and Isabella, they replied: "Show us the money," so he promised to bring back lots of gold and to convert the Chinese to Catholicism. He also wanted to become the ruler of this new land, which the king and queen refused, just in case he really did end up sharing Dim Sum with the Great Khan. Besides, that would have been like Neil Armstrong saying that the moon belonged to him.

So, when he finally set sail with three ships from Spain in 1492, it was on the understanding that he was bonkers, but that if he did discover a new continent, he couldn't keep it. After stopping off at the Canary Islands for a few weeks, he struggled across the Atlantic and reached an island in the Bahamas which he christened San Salvador which, roughly translated, means "Holy Saviour" or "Thank Christ for that!"

With a keen sense of irony and no doubt eager to be rid of their new visitors, they gave him a handful of tobacco leaves and directed him to Cuba, but Columbus crashed his ship on December 25 at Hispaniola (the Dominican Republic) and was forced to build a fort using the remains of his vessel. He called it "La Navidad" which means "Christmas" or "Chris Screwed up Here!" He abandoned 40 of his men there before sailing home to present Queen Isabella with her first stogie.

The following year he returned with 17 ships and more than a thousand men. This time he found the Leeward and Virgin Islands, Puerto Rico, and Jamaica. Then he got lazy and

Then he got lazy and ordered his crew to sign a piece of paper to swear that Cuba was so big that it must be China.

ordered his crew to sign a piece of paper to swear that Cuba was so big that it must be China. He sailed back to Spain with rum and tobacco.

Two years later he set out on his third booze cruise and discovered Venezuela, but not much gold, so he was arrested for not finding much gold and sent home in chains. But he just couldn't stay away. Like an old rocker on his final comeback tour, he set sail for the fourth time on May 11, 1502, by now an old man in failing health, with obsolete ships, and a handful of loyal family members and groupies. His aim was to find the Strait of Malacca near Singapore, but his real reason was that he'd run out of tobacco. He also explored the coast of Nicaragua and Honduras, which predictably, he decided must be China.

He died in 1506 after a disappointing career in which he had not proved that the world was round, had failed to reach China no less than four times, and thanks to him, Europeans have been trying to quit smoking ever since.

Milestones in the
History of
Breasts

1.6 million B.C.

Breasts appear. They are attached to large-brained bipedal hominids and are very hairy. Homo erectus also flourishes during this era.

Circa A.D. 1300

Early forms of breast support finally appear.

1500

Corsets constrict the waist of noble ladies, pushing their breasts up and together.

1508–1512

Michelangelo is commissioned by Pope Julius II to paint hundreds of naked breasts on the ceiling of the Sistine Chapel.

1888

National Geographic begins publication.

1912

German inventor Otto Titsling invents a chest halter for opera singer Swanhilda Olafsen. Later Philippe de Brassière steals the idea and makes his fortune.

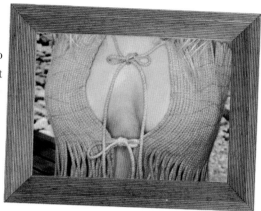

1938

The A-, B-, C-, and D-cup sizes are introduced.

1953

The first issue of Playboy is published. Sales of National Geographic fall.

German inventor Otto Titsling invented a chest halter for opera singer Swanhilda Olafsen.

1959

Ruth Handler invents the Barbie Doll which sells 351,000 units in its first year.

1962

The first breast augmentation operation takes place. It promises to be a growth industry.

1963

The bra becomes an item of male oppression, so naturally they have to come off (about time too).

1971

Feminism is exposed as a male conspiracy designed to maximize breast exposure, and bras come back on again (shame).

Feminism is exposed as a male conspiracy designed to maximize breast exposure, and bras come back on again (shame).

1989

Pamela Anderson debuts on Baywatch in "River of No Return."

1990

The world yawns as Madonna sticks two ice cream cones on her chest for her "Blonde Ambition" tour.

1994

The Wonderbra becomes a cultural phenomenon. It uses precision engineering and 54 design elements to lift and support the bust, proof that technology is finally being used for the benefit of mankind.

2004

Janet Jackson suffers a "wardrobe malfunction" at Super Bowl XXXVIII.

WERE THE CONQUISTADORS STUPID OR WHAT?

In the years preceding the Spanish arrival in Mexico, Aztec Emperor Montezuma II and his subjects were already quaking in their moccasins. They were a simple people who believed in the supernatural, so they were more than alarmed when confronted with a series of ill omens. A fiery comet blazed in the sky, and the temple of Huitzilopochtli, the god of war, burst into flames. Fishermen even discovered a bird with a mirror in the crown of its head, and legend has it that Montezuma looked into its reflection and saw his empire destroyed.

They had good reason to be scared. The Spanish Conquistadors of the early sixteenth century were barking mad and very greedy for gold and someone to fight. Their mission statement was *"Conquiste, baptise y robe cualquier cosa brillante"* or "Conquer, baptise and steal anything shiny."

Spain had been constantly at war for the last 800 years, driving the Moors from its soil. When this was finally achieved in 1492, the Conquistadors got wind that Columbus had just discovered a place called the New World, where the natives fought like girls. They were really jealous, since he hadn't even been looking for a new continent but bumped into it on his way to Asia. They wanted in.

The principle architects of this shameful conquest were a sickly minor nobleman called Hernán Cortés and Francisco Pizarro, the bastard son of an infantry Colonel.

They had also heard tell of a remarkable place called El Dorado, an entire city of gold, ruled over by a gold king who ate gold, bathed each day in his golden lake, and wiped his backside with gold triple-ply.

They never found it, but they also failed to notice a remarkable treasure that has since been discovered by archaeologists excavating along Brazil's Tapajos River. The locals call it terra preta and it holds the key to how ancient peoples mastered the subtle art of soil alchemy that baffles modern agriculturists. They actually grew the stuff. Soil, that is.

By burning down the rain forest and then adding organic matter and mixing in the charcoal from the trees, ancient tribes were able to create a nutrient-rich loam that renews itself. This is very different from the unsustainable slash and burn methods used today. Today, locals dig it up to sell, but as long as they leave about eight inches of terra preta undisturbed, the soil regenerates over a period of about 20 years thanks to a delicate combination of bacterial and fungal activity.

The Conquistadors may not have found El Dorado, but had they looked under their feet, they might have discovered a secret that, when harnessed by modern humankind, could prove to be more valuable than the shiny stuff.

Fat Chicks:
A HISTORICAL PERSPECTIVE

If you think your year six history teacher was the fattest chick in history, you'll be surprised to learn that women have been waddling around in the history books for centuries.

Men have always desired what they can't have. It's debatable whether impoverished males drooled over weighty women more for their nutritional content than their conspicuous display of wealth but there is no denying that back then, flesh was flash.

Simonetta Vespucci

Known as "La bella Simonetta" during her lifetime and easily a size 18, she was the hottest date in fifteenth-century Florence. Once the Italian painter Sandro Botticelli got a look at those curves, he painted no one else for the rest of his career. She was the inspiration for the Birth of Venus (1485) and a host of other priceless masterworks. Her face was also used for the Virgin Mary in his religious paintings. But Botticelli wasn't the only artist fawning over her folds. Countless poems and paintings were dedicated to her. She was also believed to be the mistress of Prince Lorenzo de Medici.

Titian's Venus

Titian (1485–1576) is generally acknowledged to be the greatest painter of fatties who has ever lived. Big bones were never more desirable than in the High Renaissance. Check out Venus of Urbino (1538), Venus with Organist and Cupid (1548), and Venus with a Quarter Pounder and Large Fries (c. 1555).

Hélène Fourment

She was the hefty wife of Baroque master Peter Paul Rubens (1577–1640), who fell for her charms when she was just a tubby teenager. His Venus Before a Mirror (1615) ranks as one of the most beguiling homages to neck wattle and cellulite ever committed to canvas. She was so fat, even Jakob Fugger the Wealthy couldn't have paid for her liposuction.

Boucher's Nudes

After the Baroque came the Rococo Era in which Francois Boucher, court painter to Louis XV, made his mark with endless representations of fuller-figured ladies lolling around in mythological paradises ordering extra mayo on the side. See Nude is a Sofa (1752) and The Visit of Venus to Ann Harvey (1754). Boucher was hugely criticized for his decadence by the likes of Diderot who despised voluptuousness (read: the well-fed aristocracy) for its own sake. For the first time we begin to see a devious connection developing between lard and lax morals.

Lady Hamilton

Born poor white trash, she was so beautiful that she eventually married into the nobility. She is most famous for being the mistress of Lord Nelson. She let herself go in her later years, (see Lady Hamilton as a Bacchante, 1792, in which she resembles a corpulent Alanis Morrisette) but this

Born poor white trash, she was so beautiful that she eventually married into nobility.

did little to dent her status as the horniest woman in Europe.

Doña Isabel Cobos de Porcel

Goya's painting of her in 1806 is one of the most universally admired works of the Romantic Era. Weighing in at more than 200 pounds, she looks like she could eat a human being for breakfast and still have room for a BLT.

WHICH OF HENRY VIII'S WIVES WAS THE MOST BEDDABLE?

Catherine of Aragon

The youngest daughter of Ferdinand and Isabella of Spain. Despite bearing a striking resemblance to the founder of early-eighties synth-pop, Howard Jones, the Spanish princess was considered a great beauty. Henry's first boyhood crush may well have been on Catherine, since she originally married his older brother Arthur when Henry was only ten years old and she was fifteen. He must have had mixed feelings when Arthur died six months later: sad that his brother was dead, while at the same time knowing that as soon as he was fourteen his dad would pair them off. He must have been counting down the days only to be forced to renounce his betrothal in 1505 when his father went cold on the idea of an English/Spanish alliance. When his father died in 1509, one of the first things Henry did was marry Catherine. She was 23 and he was two weeks off his eighteenth birthday and had probably been pining away for eight years waiting for that moment.

Sadly things went downhill over the next two decades. She couldn't provide him with a male heir (despite 15 pregnancies resulting in one daughter, Mary), and this led to Henry denouncing the power of the Pope in England (who wouldn't grant an annulment) so that he could marry the sister of one of his mistresses whom he had knocked up in 1533. Her name was Anne Boleyn.

Anne Boleyn

By now Henry was 42 and Anne was 26. He had been trying to get her into bed for seven years. A quote from the Venetian Ambassador said she was "not one of the handsomest women in the world" which must have been the understatement of the century, seeing as she had six fingers on one of her hands and a large goiter on her neck. The contemporary "ideal" of beauty was blonde hair, blue eyes, and a goiter-free neck. Anne was swarthy with dark brown hair and eyes. But clearly Henry's passion for Anne was real. Seventeen of his love letters to her are kept in the Vatican library—and Henry hated writing. The real reason for his desire was predictable: she wouldn't let him into her corset. For her it was queen or nothing.

She gave him a daughter, Elizabeth I, but never managed a male heir, so Henry trumped up charges of adultery, incest, and plotting to murder him, and had her beheaded on May 19, 1536. Ten days later he was romping in the sack with his third wife, Jane Seymour.

Jane Seymour

Where Anne had been fiery and witty, Jane was quiet and meek. However, whereas Anne had most likely withheld sexual favours as part of a cunning rise to power, plain Jane was a good girl who wanted to do the right thing. It was probably this demure innocence that stirred Henry's passion. She was the wife who famously gave Henry the heir he so badly wanted, Edward, but she died twelve days after giving birth. Henry stayed single for a whole two years after her death before marrying again.

Anne of Cleves

By now Henry had married his boyhood crush, a sassy temptress and a good girl. Wife number four was more for political reasons: an alliance with France. He sent Hans Holbein, probably the most famous of the Tudor painters, to the court of the Duke of Cleves to check her out and paint her portrait, to make sure she wasn't a complete hound. But by the time the marriage took place on January 6, 1540, Henry was already looking for a way out. He infamously referred to her as a "Flanders mare" and told courtiers and ambassadors that he couldn't bear to lay her because of her appearance. Besides the 49-year-old already had the hots for the 16-year-old Catherine Howard.

Catherine Howard

Being one of Anne Boleyn's cousins, you'd think she would have been careful not to arouse Henry's suspicions of infidelity. But alas, she was a stupid and flirtatious teenager married to a morbidly obese and often bedridden despot in decline. She was beheaded on February 13, 1542, after barely 17 months of marriage.

Katharine Parr

The one who survived. At 32 she was Henry's oldest wife. She was tall, lively, and witty, with a kindly and sensible nature. This time he was determined she would remain faithful, so he passed a law making it a treasonable offence for anyone who knew and didn't reveal details of infidelity within the royal marriage. But she was more of a companion and nursemaid than a lover though they did consummate their marriage on several occasions. She combined beauty with intelligence and it was her brains and learning that almost got her branded a heretic, but also enabled her to talk her way out of trouble.

WHAT WAS SO TERRIBLE ABOUT IVAN?

Ivan the Terrible, the first Russian czar, was born in 1530. He came to the throne at the age of three after his father's death. When he was seven his mother was poisoned. At this young age, Ivan was already showing early signs of being a violent freak. Like most despots, he seems to have enjoyed torturing animals as a child—he used to throw them from tall towers and watch them splatter on the ground below.

Ivan's early years of rule were unusually peaceful and productive. First off he held a national virgin competition and chose his wife, Anastasia Romonov, whom he genuinely cared for. He appointed an advisory council, established a standing army, subordinated the church to the state, and annexed a few places (Kazan, Astrakhan, and Siberia)—all pretty standard stuff for a young ruler seeking consolidation of his power base and the expansion of an empire.

Things began to go to pot when Ivan's best friend and advisor Andrei Kurbsky defected to the Poles, and his wife was poisoned in 1560. When she was alive, she had kept his violent impulses in check, but he spent the rest of his life torturing his enemies in the most gruesome ways. His favourite hobby was trying to invent and recreate the pains of hell in conjunction with his newly formed secret police, the Oprichniki, whom—in suitably fetishist style—he dressed up as monks. He especially favored roasting victims on a spit and holds the world record for the highest number of people squeezed into a giant skillet.

Ivan's early years of rule were unusually peaceful and productive. First off he held a national virgin competition and chose his wife.

Ivan tortured an entire city—Novgorod—and then butchered between 30,000 and 60,000 innocents in a week-long orgy of violence. He also exiled thousands of nobles to destroy their influence, which fragmented the whole country and left it weak and divided after his death.

Before his death, Ivan conveniently repented, took monastic orders, and was buried in a monk's habit. He had already stabbed his eldest son to death in a violent rage two years earlier, so his dynasty ended with his mentally subnormal son Feodor, who never married.

TULIPMANIA

If the South Sea Bubble has ever caught your imagination as one of the famous biggies in the annals of stock market stupidity and lost fortunes, then you may be interested to learn that about 100 years earlier, Holland had its very own speculative disaster, and all over a bunch of flowers.

For centuries the tulip has been one of Holland's most famous assets, but the Tulipomania in the early seventeenth century is one of the saddest episodes in her economic history and a warning to anyone considering doing anything more than wave at a passing bandwagon.

In 1593 a Dutch botanist called Carolus Clusius went on vacation to Turkey, and instead of bringing back the usual souvenirs (a carpet, a hookah, and an alabaster chess set), he opted for a handful of tulip bulbs. He planted them in his garden—the first tulips Holland had ever seen. Their exotic beauty, rich colours,

Dutch botanist Carolus Clusius went on vacation to Turkey, and instead of bringing back the usual souvenirs, he opted for a handful of tulip bulbs.

and elegant simplicity soon made them popular accessories in the homes of the well-heeled.

A healthy trade in importing and growing tulips developed over the next few decades, but soon it spiralled out of control. By the mid-1630s, people were staking their houses and their life savings to buy bulbs to sell on to other gullible speculators. Everyone in the country went mad with lust for what had become a must-have-even-if-we-don't-have-anywhere-to-live object of desire.

Inevitably the bulb bubble burst in 1637 when a group of merchants couldn't sell their bulbs at the price they wanted. Rumour spread, confidence dropped, and the ensuing selling chaos bankrupted thousands, including many of the richest people in the country. E. E. Cummings once said, "The earth laughs in flowers." On this occasion the ground must have been quaking at the folly of humankind.

UGLY PEOPLE
THROUGHOUT THE AGES

In every generation certain individuals appear who force us to question our aesthetic sensibilities and have us stumbling for a paper bag; they possess that unique quality which distinguishes them from the rest of their contemporaries: grotesque ugliness. Some of them are shunned, others manage to get laid very frequently despite their appearance, but they all win a place in the history books as the most physically unappealing individuals of their generations.

Socrates, the Greek philosopher dude from Bill and Ted's Excellent Adventure, was famous for having a face like a pig's with a pug nose and little piggy eyes. A Greek face-interpreter expert "read" his face and predicted that he was a drunkard and a brute—Socrates agreed with him.

The notorious barbarian, **Attila the Hun** *(see page 28)*, was very short and ugly. Being king of the Huns, ugliness didn't stop him from having 12 wives, and it instilled fear into his opponents, so probably helped gain his fearsome reputation as warrior—that and being a deranged knee-biting psychopath, of course.

The European **Hapsburg** kings and queens of the sixteenth to the nineteenth centuries had large noses and the famous over-grown "Hapsburg jaw" (mandibular prognathism) due largely to their excessive interbreeding. The deformity is so pronounced that it even appears on coinage (e.g., Leopold VI the "Hogmouth" in the seventeenth century).

The wife of British king George III was **Queen Charlotte** of Mecklenburg-Stretz, and she was such a dog that it was a court joke that the king's attacks of madness were brought on by the stress of bedding her. When they were in public, she was jeered by the crowds who called her "pug-face." Because she couldn't speak any English, the courtiers were able to persuade her that they were paying her compliments.

Dance Pinx.

FREDERICK NORTH.
EARL OF GUILDFORD
O.B. 1792

Frederick North, who was British Prime Minister in the late eighteenth century, had more than his fair share of whacks from the ugly stick. He was reputed to be the ugliest man in London. He suffered from dropsy and bad water retention as well as being very fat. As if that weren't enough, he rarely washed (mind you, hardly anyone did then, but he was worse than most).

THANKS FOR NOTHING:
THE LEGACY OF THE MAYFLOWER

Thanksgiving is much more than turkey and football. It celebrates the escape from persecution of a handful of European religious dissidents who proceeded to dish it out to the Native Americans in New England.

On November 11, 1620, 102 Puritan exiles landed their ship the Mayflower at Provincetown, Massachusetts. They weren't met by any native people because they had already been killed off in large numbers by the sexually transmitted diseases that an earlier British expedition had left behind in 1614.

Undaunted, the Puritans sailed down to Plymouth Rock and built their colony, Plymouth Plantation, near the deserted and ruined Indian village of Pawtuxet, and survived on abandoned cornfields that had gone to seed. Squanto, a Native American ex-slave of an earlier English expedition, taught them that praying alone wouldn't create a harvest—they actually had to dig holes and plant corn. That first year he helped them cultivate 20 acres that kept them alive.

Squanto even helped the pilgrims to negotiate a treaty with the Wampanoag tribe, which they calculated would give them a clear 15 years to invite boat loads of settlers until they had enough of them to start kicking the natives off their land. After all, didn't Psalm 2:8 say, "Ask of me, and I shall give thee, the heather for thine inheritance, and the uttermost parts of the earth for thy possession"?

To celebrate this treaty and the first harvest of 1621, the colony's governor William Bradford announced that there would be a three-day feast. He invited the Wampanoag Chief Massasoit, as a token gesture. But the Chief, being a hospitable person, assumed the invitation had been extended to his people and so he turned up with about 90 friends and family—after all, they knew all the good songs. There was no turkey, cranberry sauce, or pumpkin pie—just corn and a rather awkward atmosphere. Needless to say, the "Indians" weren't invited round again.

THE FRENCH REVOLUTION

At the beginning of the eighteenth century, one of the major stresses in France was that there were too many French people living there. Many "enlightened" peasants felt this was an intolerable situation, so they decided to have a revolution to sort it out.

While there was no shortage of people, there was a chronic lack of French bread. For years bakers had been short-changing peasants into thinking they were getting more dough for their dough by making loaves successively longer and longer. Marie Antoinette tried to expose the scam when she famously said "let them eat cake," but her remarks were misinterpreted and became one of the prime causes of civil unrest.

Impugning the reputation of a monarch's wife has always been an effective Republican tactic (Louis XV's mistress, the so-called Countess du Barry, was pilloried in the same way). So it was no surprise that the Hapsburg Marie Antoinette, wife of

Louis XVI, should have become a target of the anti-monarchists. Her public image was of a greedy woman seduced by sybaritic pursuits, culminating in 1786 in the infamous "Affair of the Necklace." Also, many felt France should be fighting Austria rather than striking alliances with it.

A third reason for revolution was the shortage of jobs. Most workers were agricultural day-labourers desperate for work and living on or below subsistence level. Meanwhile the aristocracy were prancing around in powdered wigs that resembled enormous piles of croissants—the irony of which couldn't have escaped the censure of the ravenous peasants; they could only look on with envy as Louis XVI and his court spent their days drinking watered-down wine, eating Camembert, and rolling little metal balls across the floor.

The nobles wore short breeches, so sections of the revolting masses named themselves the sans-culottes to emphasize that their own trousers were the genuine

While there was no shortage of people, there was a chronic lack of French bread.

article. Hence, the revolution was based on France's three abiding passions: food, fashion, and Boules (the game where French men get to play with their little balls).

One of the key moments of the revolution was the Storming of the Bastille, a grim Parisian state prison and a despised symbol of despotism. July 14 is now a state holiday on which the French proudly celebrate the liberation of seven criminals and the butchering of a handful of royalist soldiers who had already raised the white flag. The Bastille was demolished to make way for an important lawn.

Today there's certainly no shortage of wine and bread, and French people enjoy the shortest working hours in Europe. Baguettes are now a standard length of 70 centimeters (in accordance with European Economic Community regulations).

One of the key moments of the revolution was the Storming of the Bastille, a grim Parisian state prison and a despised symbol of despotism.

Over the last three centuries, the population has tripled from 20 million to just under 60 million.

Today there's certainly no shortage of wine and bread, and French people enjoy the shortest working hours in Europe.

So, arguably the French Revolution was only a partial success. What did it achieve? Initially, France swapped an effete and harmless king for a much hairier but despotic emperor. However, in the long-term she gained the European Working Time Directive and ludicrous agricultural subsidies. From Caen to Cannes, the air is now filled with the languid sounds of French farmers enjoying three-hour lunch breaks, drinking pastis, and playing petanque.

NAPOLEON: IDEOLOGUE, OPPORTUNIST, OR ANNOYING LITTLE CORSICAN?

Napoleon Buonaparte was born in Corsica on August 15, 1769, with a redundant "u" in his name which he later removed. His impetuosity was apparent at birth—he was allegedly born so quickly while his mother was returning from Mass, that she didn't have time to climb into bed and whelped on an inexpensive Greek souvenir, a floor mat depicting the heroes of Homer. She named him "Napoleon," which means "cheap floor mat."

He must have been a demanding child because his parents sent him off to Parisian military school at an early age. He flunked his exams, coming in near the bottom out of sixty graduates in 1785 and was once described by one of France's leading politicians as "a little Corsican soldier of no account, who will give no trouble to anybody." Clearly he failed to recognize a small man complex when he saw one.

Napoleon then returned to Corsica to flirt with the idea of restoring its independence, but most likely to borrow money from his parents. His feelings of inferiority on account of his short stature (he was 5 foot 2 inches) were already apparent in his habit of approaching tall people and asking them, "What's the weather like up there?" He irritated the hell out of the Corsican nationalist Paoli, and his whole family fled to Marseille in 1793.

He claimed his first military victory in the same year by recapturing the city of Toulon from the British, but the Toulon citizens were all royalists and wanted to give away their city (a perennial French trait, which

He must have been a demanding child because his parents sent him off to Parisian military school at an early age.

Napoleon, being a foreigner, didn't understand). So he must have really annoyed them too. Before long, he was briefly imprisoned for hanging out with the younger brother of the fanatical republican Robespierre.

Inevitably he married above himself, both socially and physically. He seems to have been more besotted with the aristocratic Josephine de Beauharnais than she was with him. Two days after his wedding he was packed off to Italy in command of the French army over there. He defeated the Austrians and returned to France a hero. But the Directory (France's executive power between 1795 and 1799) got rid of him again by sending him to conquer Egypt and disrupt British shipping there. His navy got hammered by Nelson at the Battle of the Nile, so he abandoned his army and returned to Paris in 1799 where a coup made him one of the three ruling consuls in the new government.

The following year saw him crossing the Alps to surprise the Austrians, a tactical disaster which was only rescued by the arrival of General Louis Desaix's reinforcements. In 1803 he crowned himself Emperor and threw a huge expensive celebration which cost more than he'd raised the previous year by palming off Louisiana on the Americans. He planned an invasion of England, but his fleet was destroyed at the Battle of Trafalgar in 1805. Nevertheless, he already controlled the rest of Western Europe and imposed economic sanctions (called the Continental System) on British colonial exports (coffee, sugar, tobacco, cocoa, and cotton George III tea towels). Spain's refusal sparked off the Peninsular War, draining Napoleon of huge resources so the land of olive trees, sun, and sea soon became known as his "Spanish ulcer."

In 1810 he had his marriage to Josephine annulled because they hadn't produced an heir and wed an 18-year-old Austrian archduchess, Marie Louise. She produced a son to whom Napoleon gave the unassuming name, "King of Rome."

The Continental System was further threatened when Czar Alexander broke the British trade embargo by importing six Spode dinner plates and a giant teddy bear dressed as a Beefeater (security guard to the English royal family). In 1812, Napoleon's Grand Army entered Russia to teach Alexander a lesson he wouldn't forget, but wasn't prepared for the deadly

Russian winter which decimated his army. Napoleon abandoned his soldiers again and rushed back to Paris to raise another army.

He was finally defeated by a coalition of European forces at Leipzig in 1814 and exiled to the isle of Elba. He escaped the following year, sneaked into France, and raised yet another army in the period known as the Hundred Days, in a last ditch attempt to conquer Europe. Following his defeat by Wellington and Blucher at Waterloo in 1815, he was exiled to Saint Helena, an even more remote island in the South Atlantic, where he died in 1821, without an army.

ENGLISH KING, 24, IMPALED IN A GLOUCESTERSHIRE BATHROOM

Elvis Presley wasn't the only king to die while answering the call of nature. Monarchs have been expiring in unusual circumstances for centuries.

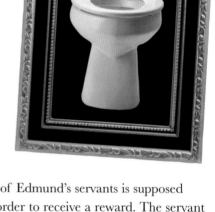

Edmund II (992–1016) He gained the nickname "Ironside" for his ferocious defence of England against the Danish king Canute. One of Edmund's servants is supposed to have murdered him in order to receive a reward. The servant wedged a sharpened wooden stake in the royal bathroom at Minsterworth in Gloucestershire and when the king sat down on the throne, the servant blew out the candle, causing Edmund to impale himself in the dark, though other reports claim he hid under the toilet and stabbed the

Elvis Presley wasn't the only king to die while answering the call of nature.

king twice where the sun don't shine. When the servant approached Canute's court for his reward he was hanged from the highest oak the Danes could find.

George II (1683–1760)

On October 25, 1760, the King of Great Britain, France, and Ireland, Defender of the Faith, Dei Gratia, Magnae Britanniae, Franciae et Hiberniae Rex, and Fidei Defensor, died from a stroke shortly after breakfast while straining on the toilet.

Edmund of East Anglia
(841–869)

A tall fair-haired hunk, this popular king was murdered by the Vikings for being a Christian. He was tied to a tree, whipped repeatedly, then shot so full of arrows he is said to have resembled the holy martyr Sebastian. He was then beheaded and his torso was thrown into a gorse bush while his head was hidden in the woods, where it kept calling "I'm over here!" until his loyal subjects discovered it between the paws of a huge tame wolf, which had been protecting it from the other wild animals. He was given a Christian burial and is now a saint with a shrine at Bury St. Edmunds, Suffolk in England and a feast day of November 20.

Sigurd I of Orkney (d. 892)

According to an Icelandic saga, Orkneyinga Saga, Sigurd was the first Earl of Orkney. It describes how he duped and killed an opposing Scottish Earl with buck teeth called Maelbrigte Tusk, chopped off his head and strapped it to his saddle so that he could ride home to show it off. One of the teeth punctured his leg, the wound became infected, and he later died. The Orcadians were so incensed that they kicked the head around the island. This is the legendary origin of the Kirkwall Ba' game which takes place today on Christmas Day and New Year's Day every year on Orkney. Teams are decided by birthplace: anyone born north of the Cathedral is a "Doonie" everyone else is an "Uppie." Needless to say, a ball is used instead of a human head.

Harald I of Orkney (d. 1131)

The Orkneyinga Saga also tells of co-earls Harald and Paul. Harald's mother Helga and her sister Frakokk made a white linen robe as a poisoned Christmas present intended to kill Paul. When Harald saw it he was so jealous that he snatched it from them and tried it on. Then "his flesh started to quiver and he began to suffer terrible agony." He took to his bed and died. When Paul found out he banished the two women to Sutherland. Talk about overreacting.

Then "his flesh started to quiver and he began to suffer terrible agony." He took to his bed and died.

Edward II (1284–1327)
The arranged marriage of the inept and unpopular king Edward II of England and Isabella of France hit rock bottom in 1326, when she captured his gay lover Hugh, had his genitals cut off and burned them before his eyes before decapitating him. The following year she arranged for Edward to be killed by having a red hot poker shoved up his backside at Berkeley Castle in Gloucestershire. He was the first English king to be deposed (and disemboweled) since the Norman Conquests.

FLORENCE NIGHTINGALE:
LESBIAN LADY OF THE NIGHT?

The Lady of the Lamp was born in Florence on May 12, 1820. Her parents, who were on a two-year tour of Europe at the time, named her after this historic Italian city. Her elder sister wasn't so lucky. She'd been born the previous year while they were soaking up some rays on the Amalfi Coast and ended up with the name Parthenope, which is Greek for Naples.

Florence was one of the most educated women of her generation. Her father schooled her in the classics, and she excelled at mathematics after persuading her reluctant parents to allow her to study this "masculine" discipline. She later became the first woman to be elected a Fellow of the Royal Statistical Society.

In the nineteenth century, nursing was reputed to be a job for drunks and prostitutes, so Florence's wealthy Victorian family were mortified when she decided to follow her vocation. In reality, a nurse was under serious risk of being seduced or raped by doctors and horny medical students, which is why nurses unfairly gained a loose reputation. It was an horrific job, so it is no surprise that alcohol abuse was commonplace.

She is best remembered for her work from 1854 to1856 at the Barracks Hospital at Scutari, during the Crimean war, in which Britain, France, and Turkey fought an incompetent, though ultimately victorious, war against Russia. Florence improved sanitary conditions and survival rates for soldiers in her care. Although a hands-on and compassionate nurse, her real breakthrough came with the results of her statistical analyses, in

which she cross-referenced mortality rates and then presented them as proof that sanitation needed to be revolutionized.

So, she was a mathematically gifted woman who didn't put out, but was she gay? It is certain that she enjoyed several passionate female friendships, first with an aunt, then with her cousin Marianne Nicholson of whom she said: "I have never loved but one person with passion in my life, and that was her." Later she had a very close relationship with Mary Clarke, an Englishwoman she met in Paris in 1837. One quote is often attributed to her as conclusive proof: "I have lived and slept in the same bed with English countesses and Prussian farm women . . . no woman has excited passions among women more than I have."

That sounds a bit gay by anyone's standards, but she was a deeply religious woman living with strict Victorian mores who saw her calling to nursing much the way a nun devotes her life to God, so, sadly, it is likely that the only action she saw was military rather than Sapphic.

W HAT'S MY MOTIVATION, LOVE?

There are occasions when fate plucks ordinary folk from obscurity and offers them minor roles in the great dramas of history. While the good, the bad, and the great make names for themselves, these bit players are often unaware that they are even taking part. One such man was Edman Spangler.

He was born on August 10, 1825, in York, Pennsylvania, and was known as "Ned" to his friends. Nothing of note happened to him for the first 39 years of his life, or if it did, nobody bothered to write it down, since who could have predicted that he would become notorious when he was just a few months shy of his fortieth birthday? In fact, he was destined to perform an act so heinous that he would be sentenced to six years' hard labour for his participation in one of America's most famous crimes.

On the morning of April 14, 1865, Edman left his rented room at Mrs. Scott's on the corner of Seventh and G Streets in

Washington, DC, and walked to work as usual. He was a carpenter and stagehand at Ford's Theatre. He was in a bad mood, since he could reasonably expect to toil the skin off his knuckles in preparation for the visit of Abraham Lincoln and a group of other dignitaries that evening. He spent the morning making alterations to the State Box to accommodate the presidential entourage. This involved removing a partition to make more space and shifting furniture around. Eyewitnesses reported hearing him curse Mr. Lincoln while he was working.

At lunchtime, an actor acquaintance, John Wilkes Booth, dropped by the theatre and invited Edman and a group of his stagehands out for a drink. After lunch, probably feeling sleepy after a few stiff ones, Edman returned to the theatre to make final preparations for the president's visit. Booth had mentioned casually that he might pop by Ford's that evening.

A few hours later, the theatre was buzzing. The president was sitting in his box, and the performance of Our American Cousin was well underway. The auditorium was filled with a thousand theatregoers. Edman was backstage shifting scenery when he got a message to go to the stage door, where he met a man who had just dismounted

Booth quietly whispered, "Ned, be a darling and hold my horse, while I pop upstairs for a moment."

his horse. In the half-light he could see that John Wilkes Booth was holding out the reins to him. Before brushing past to enter the building, Booth quietly whispered, "Ned, be a darling and hold my horse, while I pop upstairs for a moment."

THE OPIUM WARS:
HOW GREAT BRITAIN CREATED A NATION OF JUNKIES AND STOLE HONG KONG FROM THE CHINESE

In the seventeenth and eighteenth centuries opium was popular in China as a remedy for diarrhea. For a country with a population of 450 million, the British East India Company was keen to gain market share in the stool medicine arena, so it soon muscled in to monopolize shipments of opium from Turkey and India.

It wasn't long before the Chinese government became concerned about the number of opium dens springing up. It seemed that wherever they turned they saw folk lounging around with little sign of rectal discomfort. But what do you know; when they looked more closely, they discovered

When they looked more closely, they discovered that people were actually smoking the stuff for fun.

that people were actually smoking the stuff for fun. No kidding. Productivity was down, the economy was collapsing, and the previously healthy balance of trade was way out of whack. China had become a nation of addicts.

So the government banned it, but that didn't stop the now-illegal trade. British traffickers merely bribed corrupt officials and shipped even larger

They had another grievance: they weren't happy that British subjects should have to obey Chinese laws.

quantities of opium until, by 1839, there were more than 2,000 tons being smuggled into China each year. Until, that is, Lin Tse-hsü, a man who could not be bought, was appointed the Imperial Commissioner at Canton. Within two months he almost completely shut down the trade, destroyed existing stocks and even wrote a polite letter to Queen Victoria asking her to "stop peddling this shit, ma'am."

The British were not amused. As the most powerful nation on earth, they felt it was their duty to continue to supply a highly addictive and illegal narcotic to another country and, after its arrival, that it was the sole responsibility of the Chinese government to suppress its use. They had another grievance: they weren't happy that British subjects should have to obey Chinese laws. For example, if a drunken British sailor killed or raped a Chinese citizen, he shouldn't have to suffer the death penalty; he should receive British justice: a good talking to or, in really extreme cases, a wedgie.

In November 1839, Chinese patience finally snapped and their junks attempted to turn back English merchant ships. To help them change their minds, the British cracked open a big tea chest of whup-ass in the form of 16 warships. The Opium Wars had begun, although the word "war" implies that the Chinese stood a chance against the vastly superior British weaponry. They were quickly trounced and humbled by the outrageous Treaty of Nanking on August 29, 1842.

In the words of the treaty, "in order to put an end to the misunderstandings and consequent hostilities which have arisen between the two countries," China agreed to give Britain "most favoured nation" status, releasing all British criminals and promising to be more sympathetic towards future Brits abroad who disregarded their laws, relaxing all

To help them change their minds, the British cracked open a big tea chest of whup-ass in the form of 16 warships.

restrictions on British trade, and handing over Hong Kong (after all, the drug dealers needed somewhere to live). The Chinese even had to pay for the war, a sum of $21 million for "expenses incurred" by the British during hostilities.

Poor old Lin Tse-hsü was sent off in disgrace to clean toilets in remote Turkestan. Meanwhile, the opium trade doubled over the next 30 years, Chinese nationals were shipped off to America and the Caribbean for slave labour, and then in 1858 Britain stitched up China a second time with the Treaty of Tientsin, which legalized opium and allowed the free and unrestricted peddling of Christianity as well.

It was around this time that Wei Yüan wrote his *Illustrated Gazetteer of the Maritime Countries* (or Seven Habits of Highly Effective Imperialist Scumbags) which urged his nation to create a modern war machine and start copying the dirty tricks of the British. If you can't beat 'em, join 'em. Little wonder that modern China has such an enormous army.

BRING ME THE HEADS OF
JOAQUIN MURIETA

If you don't know who Joaquin Murieta was, think of a cross between Zorro, the Cisco Kid, and Elvis Presley—a man with mucho tasselwork and worth more dead than alive.

In the 1850s when Benicia was still the capital of California and the Gold Rush was in full swing, the area was a seething pot of greed and racial tensions with Chinese, Native Americans, African Americans, Mexicans, Irish, French, Germans, and pretty much everyone else chasing the shiny stuff and killing each other.

Reports started to appear of a posse of thieving hombres led by a man called Joaquin. They were riding around the Sierra Nevada robbing mining camps, and by early 1853, they had already killed more than 20 people and made off with $100,000 worth of gold.

Nobody seemed able to agree who Joaquin was, let alone how to catch him, although one group of bounty-hunters claimed they had grazed his cheek with a bullet. Within months local newspapers were suggesting extreme measures to flush them out: kick all the Mexicans out of the area.

Governor John Bigles had an election to win, so he made apprehending the leader of the outlaws, whoever he was, top of his agenda. He needed the support of the miners, and if necessary he was prepared to kill a hundred Joaquins, whoever they were, to boost his support. So he offered a $1,000 reward for the top honcho, (as long as he was called Joaquin).

On May 28, 1853, a posse led by Texan Harry Love set out to kill some Joaquins. They searched everywhere and finally, after months of fruitless tracking, they ambushed a Mexican camp, chopped off a man's head, and captured two compadres (who later died trying to "escape"). The head, they decided was the real McCoy (or rather, Joaquin)—it had a moustache and a scar on the cheek—what more proof was required?

The head was preserved in a bottle of alcohol and exhibited around the state for $1 a viewing. And that is how a young Mexican came to earn more with his pickled head than he "stole" when alive.

AMERICAN PRESIDENT

REFUSES TO BE PHOTOGRAPHED IN WHEELCHAIR

Franklin D. Roosevelt was born on January 30, 1882, in New York. He always harboured an ambition to become president of the United States, as had his cousin Theodore. Not only did he achieve his dream, he was elected for an unprecedented four terms, taking a demoralized, bankrupt country and leaving it at his death, 13 years later in 1945, the most powerful nation in the world.

Today it is common knowledge that he contracted poliomyelitis in 1921 when he was 39 years old. It left him a wheelchair-bound paraplegic, long before he ran for office. In fact, on January 10, 2001, President Clinton unveiled a memorial life-size bronze statue at West Potomac Park of him sitting in a wheelchair as a testament to the true extent of his achievements. But few people realize the lengths to which Roosevelt went, firstly to partially rehabilitate himself and then to keep the extent of his disability secret from the American public.

In the 1930s disability was still much misunderstood, and polio was an especially virulent and frightening illness. It could well be argued that had he not disguised his infirmity, American history would have taken a different turn. It was two years after he was struck down that he discovered the benefits of the mineral spa in Warm Springs, Georgia, where he bathed in sulphur-rich warm waters and, more importantly, devised a strategy to pull off the appearance of walking, which later became known as "the great deception."

He used orthopedic leg irons under his trousers to keep his legs rigid and in public he always braced himself by holding on to the arm of one of his sons, or an aide, while bearing the rest of his weight through a walking stick. Everyone involved practised and exercised for months in order to perfect the illusion. But none of this could have been achieved without the tacit support of the press who agreed never to discuss his paralysis nor photograph him in his wheelchair, but pictured him instead in a chair or the back of a convertible.

He used orthopedic leg irons under his trousers to keep his legs rigid.

Roosevelt succeeded. He was soon elected governor of New York and president in 1932. Today in the Roosevelt Library there just two surviving candid photos of FDR with his wheels.

SIGMUND FREUD: THE COCAINE YEARS

On April 24, 1884, an obscure, depressed, and penniless Austrian neurologist began his relationship with a little-known alkaloid derivative of the coca leaf. He had heard that the German army was using it to pep themselves up and figured his patients might benefit from a dose or two. He wasn't breaking the law; hardly anyone had even heard of this powerful psycho stimulant, and it would be another 30 years before it became illegal. So, strictly in the interests of medical science, 28-year-old Siggy scored his first 50 milligrams of cocaine.

With characteristic Teutonic restraint he observed, "One experiences a certain exhilaration and feeling of lightness" combined with "a certain furriness on the lips and palate." Despite this understated endorsement, within two months he was calling it his "magic carpet" and pushing it on his friends, family, patients, and colleagues like pizza bagels at a bar mitzvah. He even sent some to his fiancée, Martha Bernays, "to make her strong and give her cheeks a red colour." He wrote her a letter saying:

Woe to you, my Princess, when I come. I will kiss you quite red and feed you till you are plump. And if you are forward you shall see who is the stronger, a gentle little girl who doesn't eat enough or a big wild man who has cocaine in his body.

Word spread and it wasn't long before half the medical profession was using the substance. In those early innocent years, it seemed coke could cure anything from impotency to excessive masturbation; it was also an

He had heard that the German army was using it to pep themselves up and figured his patients might benefit from a dose or two.

effective local anesthetic and it made you feel damn good, too.

Freud believed he could make his name with this wonder drug that had fallen in his lap, or up his nose to be precise, so he penned a "Song of Praise" for this miracle remedy. And why not? It made him feel happy, it made Martha screw like a weasel, and it was benefiting his patients as well. He was especially pleased with the

progress of his friend Dr. Ernst von Fleischl-Marxow to whom he had prescribed coke to help him kick his morphine addiction. Fleischl was now snorting a gram a day in preference to morphine. Was there nothing that coke couldn't do?

It wasn't until Fleischl started experiencing "coke bugs"—the feeling that you have insects crawling under your skin—that Freud conceded that maybe his panacea wasn't without its side effects. So he reached a compromise and put him on a cocktail of morphine and coke and behold, the "speedball" was born. Fleischl was doomed. He died in agony in 1891.

Subsequently, Freud went on to develop his theory of the subconscious, abandoned amphetamines, and the rest, as they say, is history. Over a period of 15 years he had stuffed half of Colombia up

But his real addiction was always nicotine. It seems that the father of psychoanalysis never made it past the oral stage.

his nose, so why didn't he get hooked? He certainly manifested a significant repertoire of neurotic dysfunctions: phobias about riding in trains, death, and about visiting Rome, doubtless magnified by his cocaine use. But his real addiction was always nicotine. It seems that the father of psychoanalysis never made it past the oral stage. He typically smoked 20 cigars a day and continued to do so even after developing early onset heart disease, mouth cancer, and having his upper palate removed. No wonder he theorized that "the aim of all life is death."

Always generous with his addictions, he was renowned for encouraging those around him to light up and even rebuked his 17-year-old nephew Harry for refusing one of his cigars: "My boy, smoking is one of the greatest and cheapest enjoyments in life, and if you decide in advance not to smoke, I can only feel sorry for you." He regularly received boxes of cigars as gifts from his patients, which may explain why he was so keen on the fledgling discipline of hypnosis: "You are feeling very sleepy . . . sleepy . . . now next time I see you you will be carrying a box of fine cigars."

Suck it and see:
THE HISTORY OF
THE VACUUM CLEANER

The history of the vacuum cleaner is a fascinating tale of head scratching and blind alleys. Today it seems ludicrous that anyone would invent a domestic appliance that takes five people to carry, or that blew rather than sucked dust, but that's just how some early models were developed.

In the nineteenth century there was an urgent need for a floor cleaning machine. Until then the only way to clean carpets was to take them outside and beat the crap out of them. Despite appealing to the more brutal aspects of late-Victorian morality, this tedious task was only performed once a year during spring cleaning.

Manually operated vacuum cleaners have been around for more than 130 years. The oldest was invented in a Chicago basement in 1869 by Ives McGaffey. He patented it as a "sweeping machine" and optimistically named it the

"Whirlwind." Only two of them survive today—one in the Hoover Historical Center in Canton, Ohio, and the other in a private collection. An advertisement for another early model shows a husband and wife sharing the task: he sits reading a newspaper in a special pumping chair while she pushes the business end around the room.

It was not until small engines appeared around 1900 that people tried using compressed air to remove the dust. All that did was blow the dirt about the room. Finally, in 1901, a lateral-thinker called Herbert Cecil Bothe made the staggering observation that it might be better to suck than blow. He built a noisy sucking machine that worked well but it was so huge it had to be parked in the road outside. He was often sued for disturbing the peace and frightening passing horses. Once he almost choked to death on a mouthful of dust during a demonstration in a London restaurant.

Until the nineteenth century the only way to clean carpets was to take them outside and beat the crap out of them.

Two of his contemporaries dreamed up variations on the same theme: Corinne Dufour invented a device that sucked dust into a wet sponge and David Kenney's monstrosity wouldn't be out of place in Fritz Lang's Metropolis. His behemoth was installed in the cellar and connected to a network of pipes leading to each room in the house. However, Bothe's superiority was confirmed when King Edward VII bought two of his cleaners after they were used to clean the carpet in Westminster

Abbey for the King's coronation in 1902. The vacuum cleaner was here to stay as inventors began to address the issue of miniaturization.

The first electric model to challenge the definition of the word "portable" was invented in 1905 by Chapman and Skinner in San Francisco. It didn't sell well, owing largely to the fact that it was heavy and cumbersome. Dragging a medium-sized aardvark around the room would have been easier and equally ineffective. Two years later, James Murray Spangler, a janitor in a Canton, Ohio, department store, rigged up an old fan motor, soap box, and broom handle with a pillow case to collect dust and invented the prototype of the first truly portable electric vacuum cleaner. One of the first buyers was his cousin, whose husband, William H. Hoover, later became the president of the Hoover Company, with Spangler as superintendent.

At a time when a new Model A Ford cost about $300, a Hoover Sweeper was around $75—a quarter of the price of a new car, in today's terms around $7,500. It was a top range luxury item, found only in homes of the super rich. Instruction booklets of the period show only

Dragging a medium-sized aardvark around the room would have been easier and equally ineffective.

uniformed domestic servants using them, and in the 1920s, Hoover owners were even portrayed as super trendy "Flapper girls." It was only in the 1950s that mass production brought an affordable Hoover vacuum cleaner into nearly every home.

HUGE ROCKS & A MOTHER COMPLEX:

THE EGO BEHIND THE MAKING OF MOUNT RUSHMORE

The story behind the faces on the most famous mountain in the world is a tale of one man's vision, colossal ego, and dogged determination. His name was Gutzon Borglum, a sculptor with ambitions beyond the reach of ordinary men. Some would say he was a cantankerous megalomaniac, others branded him an obsessive fool, but historians have long overlooked a single tragic flaw in his psyche: he had a gargantuan breast fixation.

He always maintained that his mother had died when he was five, but in reality his father, a Danish Mormon, kicked her to the curb. When he was a young man, Borglum married a woman twice his age and then spent his adult life carving monumental structures with dynamite. You don't have to be a Freudian to join the dots: the man was deprived of the comfort of the mother's breast in infancy, and then made it his life's mission to seek out the biggest rocky outcrops on the planet and blast them to smithereens.

Mount Rushmore wasn't his first foray into chiseling writ large. In 1916 he was invited to North Western Georgia to carve the face, ten feet across, of the Confederate leader Robert E. Lee on Stone Mountain, the largest slab of granite in existence. Initially he declined, saying that it would be equivalent to "sticking a postage stamp on the side of a barn." He proposed instead his own grand vision: a huge pair of knockers 200 feet high and 1,300 feet long depicting the entire Confederate army with portraits of all its leaders. It was a monumental vision at once inspired, fanatical, and completely insane.

Work began immediately but, after nine years of under-funding and feuding, Borglum was sacked for "offensive egotism and delusions of grandeur," so he destroyed his scale model and all his plans, and a warrant was issued for his arrest. The charges were later dropped, but the experience must have scarred him deeply. (Work on the Stone Mountain project continued sporadically for the next four decades until a scaled-down, but nonetheless epic, version, 90 feet by 190 feet, of President Jefferson Davis, Robert E. Lee, and Thomas "Stonewall" Jackson was finally completed in 1970.)

Borglum already had designs on Mount Rushmore. It took 17 years and cost nearly $1 million to complete the project that today attracts three million visitors every year to South Dakota to gaze in awe at the four biggest busts in the world.

WAS GANDHI ANOREXIC?

With growling stomach and soothing words, Mahatma Gandhi was never known to have raised his voice. He was one of the most respected spiritual and political leaders the world has ever seen. He brought the British Empire to its knees with his unswerving commitment to nonviolent resistance and the avoidance of snacking between meals.

More than once he used fasting to impress upon others the need to be nonviolent. When he wasn't fasting, he lived on vegetables, fruit juices, and goat's milk. Maybe it was this bland diet that urged him to commit his famous act of defiance at Dandi on April 5, 1930, when he challenged the British monopoly by picking up a small lump of natural salt, thus breaking the "salt laws" and beginning the movement of civil disobedience against British Imperialism. Inevitably Gandhi was arrested, and thousands of others were also hauled off to jail.

More than once he used fasting to impress upon others the need to be nonviolent.

The British Government were keen to discredit him and knew it would be big news if they could only catch him tossing his cookies after lunch, or bingeing on an entire packet of Oreos, but they failed, for they had underestimated this remarkable man of huge integrity and tiny portions.

On January 13, 1948, at the age of 78, he began a fast with the purpose of stopping rioting between Hindus and Muslims. He wanted them to live together in peace. After five days of fasting the opposing leaders pledged to stop the fighting. Twelve days later a Hindu fanatic, Nathuram Godse, who opposed his programme of tolerance towards the Muslims, assassinated him. As he lay dying, Gandhi blessed his assassin with the words He Ram! He Ram! ("Oh God! Oh God!").

Gandhi died as he had lived, with an open heart and an empty colon. He weighed just 112 pounds.

GREAT MOMENTS IN THE HISTORY OF FOOD

100,000 BC
Adam and Eve get kicked out of the Garden of Eden and start growing their own apples.

3,000 BC
Persians begin using colored eggs to celebrate spring.

350 BC
Greek gourmet Archestratus writes The Life of Luxury, the world's first cook book.

AD 32
Jesus Christ feeds 5,000 using five loaves and two fishes and produces 12 baskets of leftovers.

In 3,000 BC, Persians begin using colored eggs to celebrate spring.

AD 220
Roman emperor Heliogabalus kills 600 ostriches to make a pie for his grandmother.

1665

Sir Isaac Newton watches an apple fall from a tree and figures out the laws of gravity and motion.

1762

The sandwich is invented by John Montague, fourth Earl of Sandwich, who demands bread, cheese, and meat be brought to the gambling table.

Jesus Christ feeds 5,000 using five loaves and two fishes and produces 12 baskets of leftovers.

1853

George Crum, a chef at the Moon Lake Lodge resort in Saratoga Springs, invents the potato chip after a customer complains that his French fries are too thick.

1906

Four-year-old Raymond Kroc and his father visit a phrenologist who feels the bumps on his skull and predicts that he will work in the food-service industry. Forty-eight years later, working as a milk

shake machine salesman, Ray spots a hamburger stand in San Bernardino, California, and envisions a massive new industry: fast food.

Andy Warhol makes a silkscreen print on canvas of a can of Campbell's Tomato Soup.

1908

Kikunae Ikeda invents the food ingredient, monosodium glutamate (MSG) and forms a company, Ajinomoto, to produce it.

1916

Los Angeles noodle maker, George Jung, invents fortune cookies.

Today is your lucky day

1952

Mr. Potato Head hits toy store shelves and becomes an instant success, with $4 million in sales during the first year.

1962

Astronaut John Glenn eats the first meal in space—pureed applesauce squeezed from a tube aboard the Friendship 7.

1964

Andy Warhol makes a silkscreen print on canvas of a can of Campbell's Tomato Soup.

2003

McDonald's reports its first ever quarterly net loss of $344 million for the October-to-December period compared with a profit of $272 million the year before.

HOW MANY BALLS DID HITLER HAVE?

"Hitler, he only had one ball,
Goering, he had two but very small,
Himmler had something simmler,
But poor old Goebbels had no balls at all."

It is common during times of war for allied forces to raise doubts about the reproductive abilities of the enemy leaders. For example, during the recent Gulf War, the CIA started a rumor that Saddam Hussein was gay; during the Vietnam War Pol Pot was pictured on the front of Time magazine sporting a fine set of man boobs; and at the Battle of Hastings, the British forces mocked William the Conqueror for having "a manservante thinne and meane."

After a conflict it is the historian's job to disentangle the truth from the morass of misinformation and propaganda that inevitably accompanies any war. We know Hitler was nuts, but did he have just one? Did his lust for world domination boil down to gross overcompensation for his monotesticular status?

We do know that he was wounded in the Battle of the Somme during the First World War, and some sources claim it was in his thigh or groin. Losing one of his nads is not the sort of thing that Adolf would have boasted about down the Reichstag, so we must look to his autopsy for further clues. The trouble is, it was the Russians who captured the Feuhrer's bunker in May 1945, and no one in the West ever saw his body.

British historian Hugh Trevor Roper's version of events claims that Hitler

We do know that he was wounded in the Battle of the Somme during the First World War, and some sources claim it was in his thigh or groin.

and his girlfriend Eva Braun shot themselves and that their bodies were cremated. However, there were plenty who believed that he escaped to Spain or Argentina. The Russians claimed that they had performed an autopsy on Hitler's body in 1945 and, furthermore, that he was indeed minus a left testicle, despite there being no mention of his deficiencies in his medical records. It is possible that the Russian autopsy was fake, although in 1972 an eminent dental expert from the University of

A 1945 Russian autopsy claims Hitler testicularly challenged. Hitler X-rays pronounced genuine in 1972.

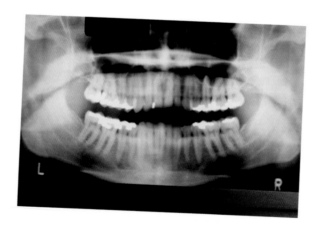

California studied the data and matched X-rays of Hitler's skull to autopsy records and pronounced the autopsy genuine.

So on balance, maybe we should accept that Hitler had merely one ball, if only because it's the most entertaining conclusion. In The Psychopathic God: Adolf Hitler (Da Capo Press, 1993), Robert G. L. Waite examines Adolf's borderline personality and holds up Hitler's left testicle, so to speak, as one of the key factors that shaped the future of Europe as we know it today.

THE COLD WAR
ACCORDING TO HOLLYWOOD

Iron curtains, post-war estrangement, the arms race, and mutual perceptions of hostile intention—oh, the Cold War was all so freaking complicated. Thank goodness Hollywood came to our rescue to simplify the issues and tell us what to think.

From Russia with Love
(1963)

After finding his feet in Dr. No, Sean Connery lays down the gauntlet for successive James Bonds. He is totally self-assured and cool but can play vulnerable too. Bond is assigned to steal a secret decoding machine and dodges in and out of SPECTRE's clutches. Q makes his first appearance, and Daniela Bianchi is meltingly sexy as double agent Tatiana

Romanova. If you want a contribution to the Cold War debate that includes booby-trapped briefcases, switchblade slingbacks, a fantastic fight sequence on the Orient Express, and a death-defying chase between a Scotsman and a helicopter, then look no further.

Red Dawn (1984)

A beautifully gung-ho endorsement of the Second Amendment and paranoid Cold War fantasy. It follows a group of U.S. teenagers who respond to a Soviet invasion of America by producing a stockpile of weapons from under their beds. They form themselves into "a well-regulated Militia" which as we all know "is necessary to the security of a free State." They then proceed to kick the Russkies from here to next Tuesday.

Thank goodness Hollywood came to our rescue to simplify the issues and tell us what to think.

This is such a cult film that it inspired the codename "Operation Red Dawn" for the raid which captured Saddam Hussein two decades later.

Rocky IV (1985)

Rocky I, II, and III were OK, but Rocky IV was awesome. Plucky Rocky Balboa comes out of retirement to show the world that self-belief, the love of a woman, and a big pile of logs is enough to defeat a Soviet one-man killing machine. Dolph Lundgren is so tall and shiny and can punch 1,400 psi with his left hand but he is no match for Sly's inexhaustible supply of flashbacks and training montages. In the ring he is exposed as a flawed giant built by committee. Is it mere coincidence that Gorbachev's policy of perestroika was unveiled the very same year that this film hit our screens?

> **Is it mere coincidence that Gorbachev's policy of perestroika was unveiled the very same year that Rocky came out?**

White Nights (1985)

Mikhail Baryshnikov plays an expatriate Russian ballet star forced to crash land on Soviet soil. We follow his relationship with Gregory Hines and their attempts to escape cultural oppression and timestep their way back to the land of the free. The result is a blend of Cold War propaganda and choreography, with not nearly enough dancing. Isabella Rosellini makes her first-ever appearance on film.

The Hunt for Red October (1990)

A superb simplification of Tom Clancy's best seller, this is way better than other underwater classics like Crimson Tide or The Land That Time Forgot because it stars Sean Connery. This time he bats for the other side (or does he?), playing the commander of a kick-ass Soviet nuclear sub. The numerous twists and turns always keep you guessing about what's going to happen next. Director John McTiernan, flying high on the success of Die Hard and Predator, gives those computer graphics guys a lesson in taut plot lines and good honest action movie-making.

TWELVE REASONS

WHY BILL GATES CAN AFFORD TO WIPE HIS ASS ON GEORGE WASHINGTON'S FACE

1936

Konrad Zuse invents the Z3—the first freely programmable computer—and develops techniques that form the basis of modern PCs, including floating point arithmetic and the yes/no binary principle. Ten years later he writes the first programming language called "Plankalkül."

1947–1948

The transistor is invented by John Bardeen, Walter Brattain, and William Shockley for which they receive the Nobel Prize for Physics in 1956.

January 1955

A Seattle attorney and a schoolteacher fall in love. Bill is born nine months later on October 28.

1958

Jack Kilby and Robert Noyce invent the integrated circuit (the IC or "chip"). By 1961 the first commercial ICs are made available by Fairchild Semiconductor Corporation.

1964

Douglas Engelbart invents an "X-Y position indicator for a display system" which he nicknames "the mouse" for his graphical user interface (GUI) or "Windows."

1968

Bill's elite Lakeside prep school buys computer time on a DEC PDP-10 owned by General Electric. Thirteen-year old Bill develops an interest in programming.

1973

Bill goes to Harvard where he meets Steve Ballmer, now Microsoft CEO.

1974–1975

Bill and school friend Paul Allen develop a BASIC software program for the Altair 8080, "the world's first minicomputer kit" which goes on sale for $400. Paul persuades Bill to drop out of Harvard and together they form Microsoft.

1981

Computer genius Gary Kildall, who had written the successful CP/M operating system, refuses to sign a nondisclosure agreement with IBM, so instead they ask Microsoft to write their first operating system. Bill comes up with MS-DOS, based on QDOS ("Quick and Dirty Operating System") which in turn had ripped off CP/M just enough to be considered legal. Microsoft keeps quiet about the IBM deal, buys the rights to QDOS for $50,000, and persuades IBM to allow them to keep the rights for MS-DOS.

1985

Windows 1.0 is born. Lawyers from Apple Computer prepare to sue Microsoft, claiming it has stolen its trade secrets (which they had copied from Xerox). But Apple needs Microsoft to continue writing software for them, so they reach an agreement: Bill gives Apple exclusive use of his Excel spreadsheet programme for a while in exchange for being able to license their operating system features in all future software applications until the end of time. Nice work.

But Apple needs Microsoft to continue writing software for them, so they reach an agreement.

1987

Windows 2.0 prompts Apple to file a lawsuit saying that Microsoft has infringed 170 of their copyrights. The court rules in Microsoft's favour on all but nine counts.

1993

Judge Vaughn R. Walker of the U.S. District Court of Northern

California dismisses the remaining copyright claims from Apple. Every year since, Bill Gates is consistently rated by Forbes Magazine as the richest person in the world.

2004

Bill's net worth compares favourably with the gross domestic product of Kuwait and he is rich enough to buy half of all the U.S. gold reserves in Fort Knox or give $42,355.26 to every single one of the 760,000 homeless people in America.

Modern-Day Marvels

The seven wonders of the ancient world included the Great Pyramid at Giza, the Hanging Gardens of Babylon, and the Mausoleum at Halicarnassus, but we have just as many, if not more, modern candidates which prove that the ancients weren't the only ones who knew how to impress.

The Concorde

It may only have been taken out of service in 2003, but "big bird" can be saluted for being the only true supersonic passenger jet of our time, capable of flying at a speed of 1350 mph (Mach 2.04). The Concorde's maiden flight in 1969 was a historic event, and 34 years later, it still has no challenger (apart from some line drawings and a twinkle in the eyes of a select

The Concorde's maiden flight in 1969 was a historic event, and 34 years later, it still has no challenger.

number of clever aeronautical engineers). With return flights from London to New York costing as much as $10,000, the Concorde was certainly not transportation for the masses, but pay peanuts and you get to fly a stuttering twin-prop.

DNA—Mapping the Human Genome

Those wily ancient Egyptians no doubt gave it a damn good go. But the times and the scientific know-how just weren't on their side. The mapping of the human genome is undoubtedly the most important scientific breakthrough known to man. Scientists have mapped the blueprint of human life, the chemical sequences for human DNA that govern our biological makeup. An understanding of this sequence can help doctors predict the illnesses that may cause our demise.

This incredible scientific achievement is now opening doors to new research and allowing examination of genetic inconsistencies that will in turn result in prevention of disease and new cures to combat diseases that were once incurable.

The mapping of the human genome is undoubtedly the most important scientific breakthrough known to man.

And you thought building pyramids was cool.

The Hubble Telescope

Our eye into our extraterrestrial backyard, the Hubble telescope was launched in 1990 to discover new scientific secrets about our universe. It orbits 375 miles above the Earth, circling our planet every 97 minutes. Like the Forrest Gump of modern day technological wonders, it just keeps trekking, having already clocked up over 1.4 billion miles in its short lifetime.

Every day the Hubble telescope delivers an incredible 10 to 15 gigabytes of new data to scientists all over the world.

Every day the Hubble telescope delivers an incredible 10 to 15 gigabytes of new data to scientists all over the world. It allows us to measure a rapidly expanding universe and answers questions that, frankly, most of us wouldn't know how to start asking.

The Hydropolis in Dubai

The Hydropolis's architectural plans alone make it a strong contender for a truly modern marvel. This one snuck into the list purely because of its structural bravado and its desire to break new records. The underwater hotel is destined to become the world's first, with 220 hotel suites submerged 66 feet below the Persian Gulf. Constructed using a combination of steel, concrete, and Plexiglas, the costs to build this subaquatic mecca are in excess of $550 million. Access to the 835,000-square-foot, jellyfish-shaped hotel is by train through an underwater tunnel. Each room comes complete with a resident bad-ass evil dictator and emergency sub. Now we know where the new future SPECTRE headquarters will be based.

A N INCOMPLETE HISTORY OF THE
SEXUAL REVOLUTION

1863
Karl Heinrich Ulrichs self publishes *Vindex* (Vindicator), and *Inclusa* (Inclusive), the first books in modern history to address homosexuality in a positive way; he becomes the first gay activist.

1886
Richard Krafft-Ebing publishes *Psychopathic Sexualis*, discussing a whole bunch of sexual oddities including cross-dressing women and men getting off on sniffing women's gloves.

1897–1910
Henry Havelock Ellis writes his six volume *Studies in the Psychology of Sex*, depathologizing many aspects of sexuality, such as masturbation, and promoting sexual liberation (the books are banned for several years).

1903
The first nudist colony opens in Germany.

1920s
Margaret Sanger campaigns to legalize birth control and opens the first birth control clinic.

1923
Woman's Physical Freedom by Clelia Mosher discusses women's health and dismisses many Victorian myths about sexuality. It discusses the restrictive and distorting nature of corsets, positive attitudes towards menstruation, and orgasms.

1948 and 1953
After interviewing 17,000 men and women, Alfred Kinsey publishes his massive studies on the sex lives of men and women with startling results.

1953
The first issue of *Playboy* is published.

1960
Lines (of mainly men) stretch beyond sight outside bookshops as *Lady Chatterley's Lover* by D.H. Lawrence finally goes on sale after being banned in the United Kingdom for 31 years.

1962

Men all around the world melt into their armchairs, slobbering by the radio or over the TV set, while listening to Marilyn Monroe's rendition of "Happy Birthday, Mr. President."

1966

William Masters and Virginia Johnson publish the first serious study of the physiology of sexual arousal and female orgasm.

1960s to 1970s

Straight hair, tight clothes, panty girdles, and high heels are replaced by long, flowing or curly hair, Afros, sandals, jeans, boiler suits, miniskirts, or hot pants. Bras become optional.

1969

Gay guys in a bar in New York's Greenwich Village resist a police raid on June 29. The "Stonewall Inn riots" lead to the founding of the gay liberation movement.

1971

Germaine Greer's *The Female Eunuch* is published.

It's a landmark in the history of the women's movement and continues to be upheld as one of the most powerful modern studies of feminism.

1973

Betty Dodson organizes the first National Organization for Women (NOW) Conference on Women's Sexuality to familiarize women with exploring their bodies.

AND FINALLY, SOME HISTORIC ANOMALIES

If **Alfred Nobel** was so interested in peace, why did he invent gunpowder?

If **Elvis** died, explain to me how he served me in Dunkin' Donuts on Saturday night?

What did people go back to before the invention of the drawing board and what was the best thing before **sliced bread**?

Why did the **Germans** invent the railroad car 275 years before the invention of the steam locomotive?

Why did **Mussolini** invade Abyssinia? What would he have done with it?

Why didn't **Achilles** wear heel-protectors?

How come the **Romans** spent hours every day bathing scrupulously and then wiped their behinds with a communal toilet brush?

Why did Founding Father **Benjamin Franklin** begin his

last will and testament with the words, "I, Benjamin Franklin, Printer…" Did his other achievements slip his mind?

To get to sleep at night did **Genghis Khan** count heads on sticks instead of sheep jumping over fences?

Neville Chamberlain, British Prime Minister at the outbreak of WWII, held up his "piece of paper" declaring to the British people that he and Hitler had averted an impending war. Did he not stop to think that Hitler, one of history's least trustworthy characters, might have been trying to pull a fast one?

A

Achilles, 15-16, 18-19, 140
Alexander the Not-So-Great, 18-21
Alexander VI, Pope, 45
Anderson, Pamela, 60
Anne of Cleves, 70
Apollo, 40
Archestratus, 116
Aristotle, 20
Athena, 14, 40
Attila the Hun, 28-29, 76

B

Barbie doll, 59
Bezerkers, 27
Boleyn, Anne, 53, 69
Bonaparte, Napoleon, 84-87
Borglum, Gutzon, 112-113
Botticelli, Sandro, 64-65
Boucher, Francois, 66
Breasts, 58-61
Brown, Louise, 40

C

Caligula, 22-23
Catherine of Aragon, 68-69
Chamberlain, Neville, 141
Charlotte, Queen of Mecklenburg-
    Stretz, 77
Chastity belts, 42-43
Christopher Columbus, 54-57, 62
Cobos de Porcel, Doña Isabel, 67
Codpiece, 36-39
Cold War, 124-127
Computers, 128-131
Concorde, 132-133
Connery, Sean, 124-125, 126-127

Conquistadors, 62-63
Crum, George, 117

D

Defecation, 30-31
Dinosaurs, 10-11
DNA, 133
Dodson, Betty, 139

E

Edmund II, 88-89
Edmund of East Anglia, 89-90
Edward II, 91
Edward III, 37
Edward IV, 37

F

Female Eunuch, The, 138-139
Flagellants, 50-51
Food, history of, 116-119
Fortune cookies, 118
Fourment, Hélène, 65-66
Franklin, Benjamin, 140-141
Frederick II, 53
French Revolution, 80-83
Freud, Sigmund, 41, 104-107
From Russia With Love, 124-125

G

Gandhi, Mahatma, 114-115
Gates, Bill, 128-131
Genghis Khan, 28-29, 141
George II, 89
George III, 77
Glenn, John, 118
Goya, 67
Greer, Germaine, 138-139
Gregory IX, Pope, 44

H

Habsburg dynasty, 76
Hamilton, Lady, 66-67
Harald I of Orkney, 90
Hastings, Battle of, 34
Havelock Ellis, Henry, 136
Helen of Troy, 14-17
Heliogabalus, 52, 116
Henry VIII
    codpieces, 38
    excommunication, 46
    wives of, 68
Hera, 14, 41
Hercules, 16, 41
Hermes, 14, 40
Hitler, Adolf, 47, 120-123
Homer, 17
Howard, Catherine, 71
Hubble telescope, 133-134
Hundred Years' War, 37
Hunt for Red October, The, 126-127
Hydropolis, 134-135

I

Ikeda, Kikunae, 118
Innocent VIII, Pope, 45
Ivan the Terrible, 72-73

J

Jackson, Janet, 61
Jackson, Michael, 41
Jesus Christ 48, 116
Johnson, Virginia, 138
Julius III, Pope, 47
Jung, George, 118

K

Kinsey, Alfred, 137
Krafft-Ebing, Richard, 136
Kroc, Raymond, 117-118

L

Lady Chatterley's Lover, 137
Lawrence, D.H., 137
Leo X, Pope, 46
Leonidas, 19-20
Leprosy, 48-49
Lincoln, Abraham, 95
Louis XIV, 53

M

Madonna, 61
Mary Queen of Scots, 41
Masters, William, 138
Mayflower, the, 78-79
McDonald's, 119
Michelangelo, 58
Microsoft, history of, 128-131
Monosodium glutamate (MSG), 118
Montezuma II, 62
Mosher, Clelia, 137
Mount Rushmore, 112-113
Mozart, 41
Murieta, Joaquin, 100-101
Mussolini, Benito, 140

N

Nebuchadnezzar II, 52
Nelson, Lord, 67
Nero, 24-25
New Testament, 48
Newton, Sir Isaac, 117
Nightingale, Florence, 92-93
Nobel, Alfred, 140

North, Frederick, 77

O

Odysseus, 15-17
Olympus, 18-19
Opium Wars, 96-99

P

Parr, Katherine, 71
Paul III, Pope, 46
Pharaoh's curse, 13
Phillip II of Macedon, 18-20
Pious XII, Pope, 47
Polo, Marco, 54
Popes, corrupt, 44-47

R

Red Dawn, 125
Rocky IV, 126
Roosevelt, Franklin D., 102-103
Rubens, Peter Paul, 65

S

Sandwich, Earl of, 117
Sanger, Margaret, 137
Sexual Revolution, 136-139
Seymour, Jane, 70
Shih Hu, 53
Siddhartha, Prince, 40
Sigurd I of Orkney, 90
Sixtus IV, Pope, 44-45
Socrates, 76
Spangler, Edman, 94-95
St Francis of Assisi, 49
Stephen VII, Pope, 44

T

Temple, Shirley, 41
Titian, 65

Toilet paper, 32-33
Trojan horse, 17
Trojan War, 14-17
Tulips, 74-75
Tutankhamen, 12-13

U

Ulrichs, Karl Heinrich, 136
Urban II, Pope, 44

V

Vacuum cleaner, 108-111
Vespucci, Sandro, 64-65
Vikings, 26-27
Vitellius, 52

W

Warhol, Andy, 119
Washington, George, 128
White Nights, 126
Wilkes Booth, John, 95
William the Conquerer, 34-35

Z

Zeus, 15. 40